Crochet You!

Crochet You!

Crochet patterns for dolls,
clothes and accessories as
unique as you are

Nathalie Amiel

DAVID & CHARLES

www.davidandcharles.com

Contents

Introduction

Once upon a time in a land close to you, there was a child with skin the hues of sunlight, hair the colours of a rainbow, twinkly eyes and a smile in their heart. But the child felt lonely, so grandad decided on a special gift: a doll as unique as his precious grandchild.

He searched in faraway lands but could not find what he was looking for, so he returned home, sad and discouraged. One night, while sitting in his old rocking chair, he decided to take matters into his own hands. He picked up some yarn and a crochet hook and taught himself the art of crochet. In no time he had made his beautiful grandchild a precious and wonderful doll. The child loved the doll very much and took it along everywhere – and very soon there was a long line of children waiting next to grandad's chair for their very own doll. And grandad patiently created their dolls, each one of them different.

In this book you will find everything you need to make special dolls for those who deserve to have a doll as beautiful, unique and diverse as they are. Here you will find detailed instructions, tips, tricks and lots of useful pictures to help create your own beautiful, handcrafted heirloom dolls. You will be able to create dolls that are a little different. Maybe they have a missing limb, wear a hearing aid or glasses, use a wheelchair or crutches, need a little help breathing or feeding, or have some warrior scars. Maybe you want to make a doll that has Down Syndrome or vitiligo, or the cutest little assistance dog friend. I'm sure the special dolls you create will be loved, cherished and hugged to pieces!

Nathalie

How to use this book

You just need basic crochet skills to use this special doll-making book and create your very own precious dolls. This book is divided into separate sections that can be mixed and matched to make your dream doll.

So pick up your hook and yarn to create your basic doll body. Then go to the clothes section to make the cutest outfits and shoes for your doll. Style your doll with lots of accessories and goodies, and don't forget to give them a special friend to hold on to as well.

Important: Make sure your gauge/ tension is correct and change to a larger or smaller hook if needed!

Gauge/tension

The gauge/tension for the dolls, clothing and accessories is 4 sts and 4 rounds to measure 1.25cm (½in).

I have worked to the above gauge/tension using the hook sizes given in the patterns. However, it is important to crochet tightly to avoid holes so toy stuffing won't show through the stitches. If you tend to crochet loosely, you may need to use a smaller hook than recommended in the pattern.

The finished dolls measure 27.5cm (10¾in). However, please keep in mind that sizes may vary if you use different yarns or hooks to those mentioned in this book.

Abbreviations

beg: beginning

BLO: back loop only

ch: chain

ch sp: chain space

cm: centimetre

dc: double crochet

dc2tog: double crochet 2 stitches together

dc3tog: double crochet 3 stitches together

dec1: decrease by 1 stitch

FLO: front loop only

g: gram

hdc: half double crochet

hdc2tog: half double crochet 2 stitches together

in: inch

inc1: increase by 1 stitch

invdec: invisible decrease

mm: millimetre

RS: right side

sc: single crochet

sc2tog: single crochet 2 stitches together

sc3tog: single crochet 3 stitches together

slst: slip stitch

sp: space

st(s): stitch(es)

SW1: switch to colour 1

SW2: switch to colour 2

SW3: switch to colour 3

SW4: switch to colour 4

tr: treble

yoh: yarn over hook

[ ]: work instructions within brackets as many times as directed

*****: repeat instructions following the asterisk as directed

US/UK terminology

All the patterns in this book are written using US crochet terms. See the table below for the equivalent UK stitch names.

US TERM	UK TERM
single crochet	double crochet
double crochet	treble crochet
half double crochet	half treble crochet
treble	double treble
yarn over hook	yarn round hook
skip	miss

Useful tips

- Shape your doll while stuffing.

- When pattern says BLO or FLO at the beginning of the round, it counts for the entire round.

- Always use a piece of scrap yarn (or a removable stitch marker) to indicate the beginning of the round and move it up as you crochet.

- Try to secure your ends while crocheting; just carry those ends along your work and crochet over them for about 2.5cm (1in), then you can just cut them off. Much less weaving in later!

- Always crochet your chain stitches very loosely so it will be easy to work into them.

- When stuffing, insert small bits of stuffing at a time, this will help shape your dolls nicely and avoid overstuffing.

- Plan your magnets in advance so you don't forget to insert them while stuffing your doll.

- You can use different yarn thicknesses, but remember to adjust the size of your hooks and safety eyes too. Make sure you check your gauge and adjust your yarns and hooks to get the correct ratio!

- If you use different thicknesses of yarn, your dolls will be larger or smaller depending on the yarn you use.

Tools and materials

Here I've explained all of the equipment you'll need to create your doll. Hooks and yarn are the basic elements, but you'll also need various other tools and materials for adding details and creating the accessories.

HOOKS AND YARNS

The recommended hook size for each item is given in the pattern, although you may need to use a different hook size if your gauge (tension) is not correct (see How To Use This Book).

For all dolls, the body pieces are crocheted using 4-ply cotton yarn. I use Scheepjes Catona (100% cotton) for my dolls, because it works up beautifully and it's soft with a nice shine. It is also durable and you can spot-clean and air-dry your finished dolls as needed.

Cotton also creates a really sturdy fabric that holds the stuffing well and doesn't distort the shapes and volumes of the bodies.

The dolls' clothes are mainly crocheted using Scheepjes Catona, while in the wheelchairs, prosthesis and crutches I also use Scheepjes Twinkle to resemble the metal parts.

I also use a small amount of Scheepes Softie in some of the clothes and to make the assistance dog nice and furry.

Crochet hooks

You'll need crochet hooks in the following sizes to make the items in this book: 2mm (US B/1), 2.25mm and 2.5mm (US C/2).

Yarn

These are the yarns I've used, but you can choose any yarn to make your dolls unique and special.

- Scheepjes Catona (for dolls' bodies and for clothes); 100% cotton; 50g (1¾oz)/125m (137yds); 4-ply (fingering weight).

- Scheepjes Twinkle (for metal parts of wheelchair, crutches, prosthesis); 75% cotton, 25% polyester; 50g (1¾oz)/130m (142yds); double knitting (light worsted weight).

- Scheepjes Softie (for clothes and assistance dog); 75% polyester, 25% nylon; 50g (1¾oz)/145m (153yds); double knitting (light worsted weight).

Yarn quantities required are given in each pattern.

*It's important to get your doll's skin
tone just right, so make sure you pick
the perfect hue for your creation.*

OTHER TOOLS AND MATERIALS

I have added a detailed list of supplies you might need; you will not need all the supplies to create each doll and you will see that some of the supplies are optional.

Required

- **Toy stuffing**
  You can use any stuffing you like.

- **Tapestry needle**
  Use this to sew the arms, hair and other accessories to your dolls. Find one with a large eye and a blunt tip, so it won't split the yarn and will also fit your choice of yarn.

- **Eyes**
  Use 7mm (⅓in) toy safety eyes for your dolls and 6mm (¼in) toy safety eyes for the asistance dog. For safety reasons, if you are planning to give the doll to a small child, you should embroider the eyes using yarn instead.

- **Embroidery yarn**
  For eyebrows, lashes, sclera and glasses.

- **Wooden dowel or skewer**
  0.5mm (⅕₀in) for prosthesis and crutches and also if you prefer to use a dowel instead of wire to reinforce the neck.

- **Strong cardboard or plastic**
  For wheelchair, foot and shoe soles.

Optional

- **Wire**
  1.2mm (½₀in) thick and 1.5mm (¹⁄₁₆in) thick for the doll's frame and to make the wheelchair and glasses.

- **Jewellery pliers**
  For shaping the wire frame.

- **Blush**
  For the cheeks.

- **Safe acrylic paint**
  For freckles.

- **Magnets**
  If you'd like to be able to remove and reattach certain parts and accessories.

- **Scraps of felt**
  To hold down magnets.

- **Buttons**
  If you'd like the clothes to be removable.

- **Regular sewing needle and thread**
  To sew on felt pieces.

Very important: Please note that the dolls are only suitable for a child below three years of age if frames and small accessories are omitted and eyes are embroidered.

Making your doll

In this book you will find no colour suggestions at all. This is because you should feel free to use any colours you like for skin, hair, clothes and accessories. Make it your own, make it YOU!

Basic doll

Materials

- 2mm (US B/1) crochet hook
- Approximately 60g (2⅛oz) of Scheepjes Catona, or similar 4-ply (fingering weight) yarn, in your choice of skin tone
- Removable stitch markers or scrap yarn
- A wire frame prepared using the template included (see Templates), using 1.2mm wire and jewellery pliers to shape the wire
- Extras as needed for your doll from Other Tools and Materials

For any prosthesis, feeding/ breathing tubes, make sure you plan the accessories in advance so you don't forget to insert magnets into your doll's cheek/neck/amputated limbs/tummy while stuffing.

Let's get started!

Arms (make 2)

We'll start with the arms and set them aside to attach to the body later.

Using 2mm (US B/1) hook and skin tone of your choice, ch 5.

Round 1 (RS): Starting in second ch from hook, sc 3, sc 3 in next ch, sc 3 in opposite side of ch sts. (9 sts)

Place marker.

Round 2: Sc 3 in first st, sc 3, sc 3 in next st, sc 4. (13 sts)

Rounds 3 to 6: Sc 13.

Round 7: Invdec, sc 11. (12 sts)

Round 8: Sc 12.

Round 9: Sc 2 in first st, sc 5, sc 2 in next st, sc 5. (14 sts)

Rounds 10 to 17: Sc 14.

Round 18: Sc 3, sc 2 in next st, sc 6, sc 2 in next st, sc 3. (16 sts)

Rounds 19 to 22: Sc 16.

Round 23: Sc 4, stop the round here.

Fasten off and set aside.

Legs and body

RIGHT LEG

We'll start with the toe.

Using 2mm (US B/1) hook and skin tone of your choice, make a magic ring.

Round 1 (RS): Sc 6 in ring. (6 sts)

Round 2: Sc 2 in first st, sc 5. (7 sts)

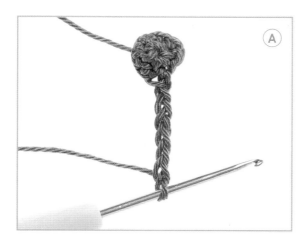

Round 3: Ch 6, starting in second ch from hook, sc 5, sc 7 around toe, sc 5 in opposite side of ch sts. (17 sts)

Place marker.

Rounds 4 to 8: Sc 17.

*You will now work in rows, back and forth, turning after each row (**do not ch 1** at beginning of row).*

Row 9: Sc 9, turn, sc2tog, sc 4, sc2tog, turn. (6 sts)

Row 10: Sc2tog, sc 2, sc2tog, turn. (4 sts)

Row 11: Sc 4, turn.

Row 12: Sc 4, sc 2 in gap between the heel and the top of foot, sc 10, sc 2 in gap between top of foot and heel. (18 sts)

Place marker. **Do not turn**, continue in rounds.

Insert cardboard sole (optional).

Round 13: Sc 5, invdec, sc 9, invdec. (16 sts)

Rounds 14 to 16: Sc 16.

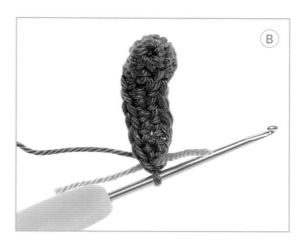

Round 17: [Sc 2 in next st, sc 7] twice. (18 sts)

Rounds 18 and 19: Sc 18.

Round 20: [Sc 2 in next st, sc 8] twice. (20 sts)

 **Rounds 21 to 24:** Sc 20.

Round 25: Sc 1, invdec, sc 3, skip 1 st, sc 3, invdec, sc 3, [sc 2 in next st] 3 times, sc 2. (20 sts)

Rounds 26 to 28: Sc 20.

Round 29: Sc 12, [invdec] 3 times, sc 2. (17 sts)

Rounds 30 and 31: Sc 17.

Round 32: Sc 3, [sc 2 in next st, sc 6] twice. (19 sts)

Round 33: Sc 7, sc 2 in next st, sc 11. (20 sts)

Rounds 34 to 41: Sc 20.

Round 42: Sc 13, stop the round here.

Fasten off, set aside.

LEFT LEG

Make second foot same as first foot through to Round 8, **turn**.

*You will now work in rows, back and forth, turning after each row (**do not ch 1** at beginning of row).*

Row 9: Sc2tog, sc 4, sc2tog, turn. (6 sts)

Row 10: Sc2tog, sc 2, sc2tog, turn. (4 sts)

Row 11: Sc 4, turn.

Row 12: Sc 4, 2 sc into gap between the heel and the top of foot, sc 10, 2 sc into gap between top of foot and heel. (18 sts)

Place marker. **Do not turn**, continue in rounds.

Insert cardboard sole (optional).

Round 13: Sc 6, invdec, sc 8, invdec. (16 sts)

Rounds 14 to 16: Sc 16.

Round 17: [Sc 2 in next st, sc 7] twice. (18 sts)

E

F

Rounds 18 and 19: Sc 18.

Round 20: [Sc 2 in next st, sc 8] twice. (20 sts)

Rounds 21 to 24: Sc 20.

Round 25: Sc 1, invdec, sc 3, skip 1 st, sc 3, invdec, sc 3, [sc 2 in next st] 3 times, sc 2. (20 sts)

Rounds 26 to 28: Sc 20.

Round 29: Sc 12, [invdec] 3 times, sc 2. (17 sts)

Rounds 30 and 31: Sc 17.

Round 32: Sc 3, [sc 2 in next st, sc 6] twice. (19 sts)

Round 33: Sc 7, sc 2 in next st, sc 11. (20 sts)

Rounds 34 to 41: Sc 20.

Round 42: Sc 4, stop the round here.

(F) Next we will connect both legs.

Make sure you hold the right and left leg in their correct place.

Round 43: Ch 2, sc 1 into first st after fastened off st of first leg, sc 19 around remainder of first leg, sc 2 along connecting ch, sc 20 around second leg, sc 2 along opposite side of connecting ch. (44 sts)

Place marker.

To stuff the legs, first stuff the tip of the foot lightly, insert the wire frame, then continue to stuff and shape your doll.

If you'd like the doll to sit, make sure you don't stuff the top of the legs at all.

BODY

Continue working in the round.

Round 1 (RS): Sc 13, sc 2 in next st, sc 3, sc 2 in next st, sc 6, sc 2 in next st, sc 3, sc 2 in next st, sc 15. (48 sts)

Rounds 2 to 7: Sc 48.

Round 8: Sc 16, [invdec, sc 1] 6 times, sc 12, invdec. (41 sts)

(G) **Rounds 9 to 15:** Sc 41.

Round 16: Sc 8, invdec, sc 3, invdec, sc 13, invdec, sc 3, invdec, sc 6. (37 sts)

We will attach the arms to the body in the next round.

(H)
(I) **Round 17:** Sc 9, sc 16 around one arm (starting after the fastened off sts), skip next 2 sts on body, sc 16, sc 16 around second arm (starting after the fastened off st), skip next 2 sts on body, sc 8. (65 sts)

Round 18: Sc 8, [invdec, sc 14] 3 times, invdec, sc 7. (61 sts)

Round 19: Sc 7, invdec, sc 14, invdec, sc 12, invdec, sc 14, invdec, sc 6. (57 sts)

Round 20: Sc 6, [invdec, sc 6] twice, sc2tog, sc 10, [invdec, sc 6] twice, invdec, sc 5. (51 sts)

Round 21: [Sc 5, invdec] twice, sc 6, invdec, sc 8, invdec, sc 5, invdec, sc 6, invdec, sc 4. (45 sts)

Round 22: [Sc 4, invdec] 7 times, sc 3. (38 sts)

Stuff the body, making sure to stuff the bottom and tummy a little more.

Stuff the arms by first inserting a tiny bit of stuffing into the doll's hands, insert the wire frame then continue stuffing the hands and arms lightly making sure to stuff the top of the arms very lightly!

Round 23: [Sc 3, invdec] 7 times, sc 3. (31 sts)

Round 24: [Sc 2, invdec] 7 times, sc 3. (24 sts)

Round 25: [Sc 1, invdec] 8 times. (16 sts)

Stuff the body some more, especially the shoulders.

Round 26: [Sc 2, invdec] 4 times. (12 sts)

Rounds 27 to 29: Sc 12.

HEAD

Continue working in the round.

Round 1 (RS): [Sc 2 in next st, sc 2] 4 times. (16 sts)

Round 2: [Sc 2 in next st, sc 1] 8 times. (24 sts)

Round 3: [Sc 2 in next st, sc 2] 8 times. (32 sts)

Round 4: [Sc 2 in next st, sc 3] 8 times. (40 sts)

Round 5: [Sc 2 in next st, sc 4] 8 times. (48 sts)

Round 6: [Sc 2 in next st, sc 5] 8 times. (56 sts)

Rounds 7 to 13: Sc 56.

Round 14: [Sc 2, invdec] 6 times, sc 32. (50 sts)

Rounds 15 to 21: Sc 50.

Remove hook from working st and replace with a removable stitch marker to prevent your sts unravelling whilst you work the face as follows:

(M) 1. Embroider the nose in the middle of your doll's face over 2 st between Rounds 12 and 13.

2. Mark out the placement of the eyes; they will be between Rounds 14 and 15 (2 rounds above the nose); there are 9 sts between the eyes.

3. For sclera and eye lashes (optional), embroider the sclera with white thread going around the lower half of the eye (see images). After you insert the eyes, they will partially cover the sclera.

4. For the eye lashes, use embroidery yarn and make two lines on the outer edge of the eyes over 2 sts, one vertically and one diagonally (see images).

5. For the eye brows, embroider a line over 4 sts, 4 rounds above the eyes slanting down 1 round; the eye brows are 8 sts apart (see images).

(N) 6. Attach your safety eyes now (see General Techniques: Attaching Toy Safety Eyes).

Your doll is going to look a little wonky at this point, but don't worry, everything will straighten out as soon as you start stuffing the head.

Replace hook into working st.

Round 22: [Invdec, sc 23] twice. (48 sts)

Round 23: [Sc 4, invdec] 8 times. (40 sts)

Stuff the head very firmly, really take your time shaping the head properly while stuffing.

Round 24: [Sc 3, invdec] 8 times. (32 sts)

Round 25: [Sc 2, invdec] 8 times. (24 sts)

Round 26: [Sc 1, invdec] 8 times. (16 sts)

Round 27: [Invdec] 8 times. (8 sts)

Fasten off, weave in ends (see General Techniques: Weaving in Ends) and close all gaps.

> *Make sure you stuff the jaw and cheeks really well and press the eye area inwards while shaping. Don't forget to make the forehead and top of the doll's head nice and round.*

(M)

(N)

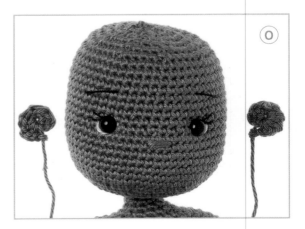

(O)

EARS

We'll make a left and a right ear as follows:

Left ear: Using 2mm (US B/1) hook and skin tone of your choice, make a magic ring.

Round 1: [Ch 2, dc 1, hdc 5, ch 1, slst] into ring.

Right ear: Using 2mm (US B/1) hook and skin tone of your choice, make a magic ring.

Round 1: [Ch 1, hdc 5, dc 1, ch 2, slst] into ring.

Sew each ear to the side of your doll's head tightly, 6 sts away from the eyes. The top of the ear will sit against Round 15.

Use some blush to colour your doll's cheeks and paint on some freckles with safe acrylic paint if you like.

Congratulations! Your basic doll is ready and now it's time to start styling.

Doll variations

Limb loss

When you're making a doll with limb loss you can adapt the pattern to make the doll exactly the way you want. Just pick the left or right leg(s)/arm(s) from the Basic Doll pattern and the left or right leg(s)/arm(s) from the limb loss pattern and then complete the doll by following the Basic Doll pattern.

You can also adapt the length of the arm(s)/leg(s) with limb loss by following the pattern below for arm(s) through to Round 5 and for leg(s) through to Round 4 and then crochet the number of rows you need to match the length of the limb.

ARM

Follow the instruction for the Basic Doll for the arm that is not amputated and then follow the instructions below for the amputated arm. Then continue with the Basic Doll pattern. If both arms are missing, follow the pattern below for both arms.

Using 2mm (US B/1) hook and skin tone of your choice, make a magic ring.

Round 1 (RS): Sc 6 into ring. (6 sts)

Round 2: [Sc 2 in next st] 6 times. (12 sts)

Round 3: [Sc 2 in next st, sc 5] twice. (14 sts)

Round 4: Sc 14.

Round 5: Sc 3, sc 2 in next st, sc 6, sc 2 in next st, sc 3. (16 sts)

Round 6: Sc 16.

Repeat the last round, until the arm is exactly as long as you want and then continue by following the Basic Doll pattern.

Legs and body

For limb loss of a leg(s) you can decide which leg(s) should be missing. Follow the instruction for the Basic Doll for the leg that is not amputated and then follow the instructions below for the amputated leg. If both legs are missing, follow the pattern below for both legs.

LEG

Using 2mm (US B/1) hook and skin tone of your choice, make a magic ring.

Round 1 (RS): Sc 6 into ring. (6 sts)

Round 2: [Sc 2 in next st] 6 times. (12 sts)

Round 3: [Sc 2, sc 2 in next st] 4 times. (16 sts)

Round 4: [Sc 3, sc 2 in next st] 4 times. (20 sts)

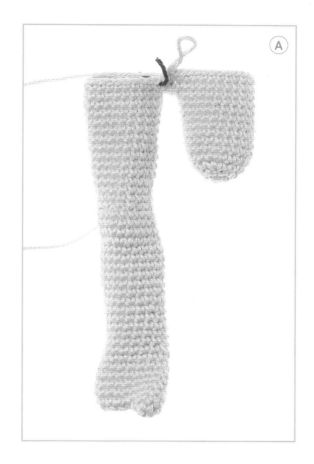

(A)—Sc 20 until the leg is exactly as long as you want it to be, then continue by following the Basic Doll pattern from Round 43.

> *When you connect both legs make sure you hold the right and left leg in their correct place.*

Stuff legs as follows:

1. Insert your magnet and stuff the amputated leg(s) lightly, then stuff the other leg.

2. Adapt your wire frame to fit the amputated leg(s).

3. Insert the wire frame, then continue to stuff and shape your doll.

Continue making the body by following the Basic Doll pattern.

> *If you'd like the doll to sit, make sure you don't stuff the top of the legs at all.*

Make sure you don't forget to insert the magnets before you stuff your doll!

Down Syndrome

Follow the Basic Doll pattern through to Round 27 of the body. (24 sts)

Round 28: [Sc 2, invdec] twice, sc 10, invdec, sc 2, invdec. (20 sts)

Rounds 29 to 32: Sc 20.

HEAD

Continue working in the round.

Round 1: [Sc 2 in next st] to end of round. (40 sts)

Round 2: [Sc 2 in next st, sc 4] 8 times. (48 sts)

Round 3: [Sc 2 in next st, sc 5] 8 times. (56 sts)

Round 4: [Sc 10, sc 2 in next st] 5 times, sc 1. (61 sts)

Rounds 5 to 13: Sc 61.

Round 14: [Sc 2, invdec] 6 times, sc 35, invdec. (54 sts)

Rounds 15 to 21: Sc 54.

Remove hook from working st and replace with a removable stitch marker or scrap yarn to prevent your sts unravelling whilst you work the face as follows:

1. Embroider the nose in the middle of your doll's face over 3 st between Rounds 12 and 13 (see General Techniques: Embroidery Stitches).

2. Place the eyes between Rounds 14 and 15 (2 rounds above the nose); there are 9 sts between both eyes.

3. For eye lids, embroider them with your skin tone. Fold yarn double, insert your needle on the bottom inside of the eye and bring it over the eye diagonally, placing one strand of yarn on either side of the eye. Do this once more and repeat for the other eye.

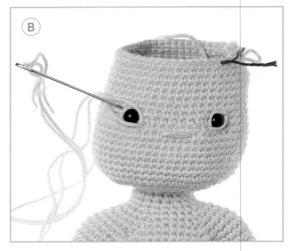

4. For the eye brows, embroider a line over 4 sts, 4 rounds above the eyes slanting down 1 round; the eye brows are 8 sts apart.

Your doll is going to look a little wonky at this point, but don't worry, everything will straighten out as soon as you start stuffing the head.

Round 22: [Invdec, sc 10] 4 times, sc 2, invdec. (48 sts)

Round 23: [Sc 4, invdec] 8 times. (40 sts)

Remove hook from working st and replace with a removable stitch marker or scrap yarn to prevent your sts unravelling whilst you stuff the head as follows:

Stuff the head very firmly, really take your time shaping the head properly while stuffing. Make sure you stuff the jaw and cheeks really well and press the eye area inwards while shaping.

Round 24: [Sc 3, invdec] 8 times. (32 sts)

Round 25: [Sc 2, invdec] 8 times. (24 sts)

Round 26: [Sc 1, invdec] 8 times. (16 sts)

Round 27: [Invdec] 8 times. (8 sts)

Fasten off and weave in ends (see General Techniques: Weaving in Ends) and close all gaps.

Don't forget to make the forehead and top of the doll's head nice and round.

EARS

We'll make a right and a left ear.

Left ear: Using 2mm (US B/1) hook and skin tone of your choice, make a magic ring.

Round 1: [Ch 1, hdc 1, sc 5, ch 1, slst] into ring and fasten off.

Right ear: Using 2mm (US B/1) hook and skin tone of your choice, make a magic ring.

Round 1: [Ch 1, sc 5, hdc 1, ch 1, slst] into ring and fasten off.

(C) Sew each ear to the side of your doll's head tightly, 6 sts away from the eyes. The top of the ear will sit against Round 15.

(D) Use some blush to colour your doll's cheeks and paint on some freckles with safe acrylic paint if you like.

For the hair, head over to the hair section. This doll's head is larger than the other dolls so the wig cap will be a little small and this is what we want. Stretch the cap over your doll's head but place the front of the wig cap on Round 23, making the forehead look bigger. Sew it on tightly and make the hair strands as desired.

Now your cutie is ready for some amazing styling!

(C)

(D)

Different sizes

You can also create dolls in different sizes by increasing or decreasing the number of stitches in the doll's legs, tummy, neck and cheeks. Make sure you adjust the stitches in their wardrobe as well so their clothes will fit perfectly.

Don't be afraid to experiment and create your doll exactly the way you imagine. Just make sure your stitches are filled with love!

Vitiligo

To create dolls with vitiligo we will use two different skin tones. We'll work with one main colour and hold the second colour behind the work throughout the entire project, switching out the colours as we go.

You can use the Basic Doll pattern and the method below to place the colour patches on your doll's skin exactly where you'd like them to be, or follow the pattern.

SWITCHING COLOUR

1. Working with the first colour, insert your hook into the next stitch, yarn over hook and pull up a loop (two loops on your hook).

Ⓐ **2.** Using the second colour, yarn over hook and pull through both loops.

3. Create as many stitches as you need, holding the first yarn behind your work, taking care not to pull the yarn tightly.

4. Then switch back to the first colour the same way, carrying the yarn you're not using behind your work. Create all the patches by switching the skin tones as needed.

Switch colour to lighter skin tone (SW1)

Switch colour to darker skin tone (SW2)

LEFT ARM

We'll start with the arms and set them aside to attach to the body later.

Using 2mm (US B/1) hook and lighter skin tone (SW1) of your choice, ch 5.

Round 1: Starting in second ch from hook, sc 3, sc 3 in next ch, sc 3 in opposite side of ch. (9 sts)

Place marker.

Round 2: Sc 3 in first st, sc 3, sc 3 in next st, sc 4. (13 sts)

Round 3: Sc 2, SW2, sc 3, SW1, sc 8.

Round 4: Sc 1, SW2, sc 5, SW1, sc 7.

Round 5: Sc 1, SW2, sc 6, SW1, sc 6.

Round 6: Sc 2, SW2, sc 4, SW1, sc 7.

Round 7: Invdec, sc 1, SW2, sc 3, SW1, sc 7. (12 sts)

Round 8: SW2, sc 7, SW1, sc 5.

Round 9: Sc 1, SW2, sc 1 in same st, sc 5, sc 2 in next st, sc 4, SW1, sc 1. (14 sts)

Rounds 10 to 13: SW2, sc 14.

Round 14: Sc 5, SW1, sc 2, SW2, sc 7.

Round 15: Sc 4, SW1, sc 3, SW2, sc 7.

Round 16: Sc 4, SW1, sc 2, SW2, sc 8.

Round 17: Sc 5, SW1, sc 1, SW2, sc 8.

Round 18: Sc 3, sc 2 in next st, sc 1, SW1, sc 2, SW2, sc 3, sc 2 in next st, sc 3. (16 sts)

Round 19: Sc 5, SW1, sc 3, SW2, s c8.

Ⓑ— **Rounds 20 to 22:** Sc 6, SW1, sc 1, SW2, sc 9.

Fasten off and set aside.

RIGHT ARM

Using 2mm (US B/1) hook and lighter skin tone (SW1) of your choice, ch 5.

Round 1: Starting in second ch from hook, sc 3, sc 3 in next ch, sc 3 in opposite side of ch sts. (9 sts)

Place marker.

Round 2: Sc 3 in first st, sc 3, sc 3 in next st, sc 4. (13 sts)

Round 3: Sc 13.

Round 4: Sc 9, SW2, sc 4.

Round 5: SW1, sc 8, SW2, sc 5.

Round 6: SW1, sc 7, SW2, sc 6.

Round 7: Invdec, SW1, sc 5, SW2, sc 6. (12 sts)

Round 8: Sc 2, SW1, sc 3, SW2, sc 7.

Round 9: [Sc 2 in next st, sc 5] twice. (14 sts)

Rounds 10 to 13: Sc 14.

Round 14: Sc 11, SW1, sc 3.

Round 15: SW2, sc 10, SW1, sc 4.

Round 16: Sc 1, SW2, sc 10, SW1, sc 3.

Round 17: SW2, sc 12, SW1, sc 2.

Round 18: SW2, sc 3, sc 2 in next st, sc 6, sc 2 in next st, sc 2, SW1, sc 1. (16 sts)

Rounds 19 to 22: Sc 16.

Ⓒ— **Round 23:** Sc 11, stop the round here.

Fasten off and set aside.

RIGHT LEG

Using 2mm (US B/1) hook and lighter skin tone (SW1), make a magic ring.

We'll start with the toe.

Round 1: Sc 6 into ring.

Round 2: Sc 2 in first st, sc 5. (7 sts)

Round 3: Ch 6, starting in second ch from hook, sc 5 in one side of ch, sc 7 around toe, sc 5 in opposite side of ch. (17 sts)

Place marker.

Round 4: Sc 7, SW2, sc 3, SW1, sc 7.

Round 5: Sc 5, SW2, sc 7, SW1, sc 5.

Round 6: Sc 3, SW2, sc 14.

Round 7: Sc 1, SW1, sc 2, SW2, sc 14.

Round 8: Sc 17.

*You will now work three rows back and forth, turning after each row (**do not ch 1** at beginning of row).*

Row 9: Sc 9, turn, sc2tog, sc 4, sc2tog, turn. (6 sts)

Row 10: Sc2tog, sc 2, sc2tog, turn. (4 sts)

Row 11: Sc 4, turn.

Continue in rounds.

Round 12: Sc 4, sc 2 into gap between heel and top of foot, sc 10, sc 2 in gap between top of foot and heel. (18 sts)

Place marker.

Insert cardboard sole (optional).

Round 13: Sc 5, invdec, sc 9, invdec. (16 sts)

Rounds 14 to 16: Sc 16.

Round 17: [Sc 2 in next st, sc 7] twice. (18 sts)

Rounds 18 and 19: Sc 18.

Round 20: [Sc 2 in next st, sc 8] twice. (20 sts)

Rounds 21 to 23: Sc 20.

Round 24: Sc 14, SW1, sc 3, SW2, sc 3.

Round 25: Sc 1, invdec, sc 3, skip 1 st, sc 3, invdec, sc 1, SW1, sc 2, [sc 2 in next st] 3 times, SW2, sc 2. (20 sts)

Round 26: Sc 11, SW1, sc 6, SW2, sc 3.

Round 27: Sc 13, SW1, sc 5, SW2, sc 2.

Round 28: Sc 14, SW1, sc 3, SW2, sc 3.

Round 29: Sc 12, [invdec] 3 times, sc 2. (17 sts)

Rounds 30 and 31: Sc 17.

Round 32: Sc 3, [sc 2 in next st, sc 6] twice. (19 sts)

Round 33: Sc 7, sc 2 in next st, sc 11. (20 sts)

Rounds 34 to 41: Sc 20.

D — **Round 42:** Sc 13, stop the round here.

Fasten off, set aside.

LEFT LEG

Using 2mm (US B/1) hook and lighter skin tone (SW1) make a magic ring.

We'll start with the toe.

Round 1: Sc 6 into ring.

Round 2: Sc 2 in first st, sc 5. (7 sts)

Round 3: Ch 6, starting in second ch from hook, sc 5 in one side of ch, sc 7 around toe, sc 5 in opposite side of ch. (17 sts)

Place marker.

Round 4: Sc 4, SW2, sc 3, SW1, sc 10.

Round 5: Sc 3, SW2, sc 8, SW1, sc 6.

Round 6: Sc 2, SW2, sc 12, SW1, sc 3.

Round 7: Sc 1, SW2, sc 15, SW1, sc 1.

Round 8: SW2, sc 17.

*You will now work three rows back and forth, turning after each row (**do not ch 1** at beginning of row).*

Row 9: Turn, sc2tog, sc 4, sc2tog, turn. (6 sts)

Row 10: Sc2tog, sc 2, sc2tog, turn. (4 sts)

Row 11: Sc 4, turn.

Round 12: Sc 4, sc 2 in gap between heel and top of foot, sc 10, sc 2 in gap between top of foot and heel. (18 sts)

Place marker.

Insert cardboard sole (optional).

Round 13: Sc 5, invdec, sc 9, invdec. (16 sts)

Rounds 14 to 16: Sc 16.

Round 17: [Sc 2 in next st, sc 7] twice. (18 sts)

Rounds 18 and 19: Sc 18.

Round 20: [Sc 2 in next st, sc 8] twice. (20 sts)

Rounds 21 and 22: Sc 20.

Round 23: Sc 15, SW1, sc 3, SW2, sc 2.

Round 24: Sc 14, SW1, sc 5, SW2, sc 1.

Round 25: Sc 1, invdec, sc 3, skip 1 st, sc 3, invdec, sc 3, SW1 [sc 2 in next st] 3 times, sc 1, SW2, sc 1. (20 sts)

Round 26: Sc 13, SW1, sc 5, SW2, sc 2.

Round 27: Sc 15, SW1, sc 3, SW2, sc 2.

Round 28: Sc 16, SW1, sc 2, SW2, sc 2.

Round 29: Sc 12, [invdec] 3 times, sc 2. (17 sts)

Rounds 30 and 31: Sc 17.

Round 32: Sc 3, [sc 2 in next st, sc 6] twice. (19 sts)

Round 33: Sc 7, sc 2 in next st, sc 11. (20 sts)

Rounds 34 to 41: Sc 20.

E — **Round 42:** Sc 4, stop the round here.

We're going to connect both legs now.

Make sure you hold the right and left leg in their correct place.

F — **Round 43:** Ch 2, sc 1 in first st after fastened off st of first leg, sc 19 more around first leg, sc 2 in connection ch, sc 20 around second leg, sc 2 in opposite side of ch. (44 sts)

Place marker.

To stuff the legs, first stuff the tip of the foot lightly, insert the wire frame, then continue to stuff and shape your doll.

If you'd like the doll to sit, make sure you don't stuff the top of the legs at all.

BODY

Continue working in the round.

Round 1: Sc 13, sc 2 in next st, sc 3, sc 2 in next st, sc 6, sc 2 in next st, sc 3, sc 2 in next st, sc 15. (48 sts)

Rounds 2 to 6: Sc 48.

Round 7: Sc 20, SW1, sc 3, SW2, sc 25.

Round 8: Sc 16, invdec, sc 1, SW1, [invdec, sc 1] twice, SW2, [invdec, sc 1] 3 times, sc 12, invdec. (41 sts)

Round 9: Sc 18, SW1, sc 5, SW2, sc 12, SW1, sc 3, SW2, sc 3.

Round 10: Sc 18, SW1, sc 4, SW2, sc 12, SW1, sc 5, SW2, sc 2.

Round 11: Sc 19, SW1, sc 3, SW2, sc 12, SW1, sc 6, SW2, sc 1.

Round 12: Sc 34, SW1, sc 5, SW2, sc 2.

Round 13: Sc 2, SW1, sc 3, SW2, sc 30, SW1, sc 3, SW2, sc 3.

Round 14: Sc 3, SW1, sc 2, SW2, sc 30, SW1, sc 3, SW2, sc 3.

Round 15: Sc 35, SW1, sc 2, SW2, sc 4.

Round 16: Sc 8, invdec, sc 3, invdec, sc 13, invdec, sc 3, invdec, sc 6. (37 sts)

We will attach the arms to the body in the next round.

Round 17: Sc 9, sc 16 around right arm (starting after fastened off st), skip next 2 sts on body, sc 16, sc 16 around left arm (starting after fastened off st), skip next 2 sts on body, sc 8. (65 sts)

Round 18: Sc 8, [invdec, sc 14] 3 times, invdec, sc 7. (61 sts)

Round 19: Sc 7, invdec, sc 14, invdec, sc 12, invdec, sc 14, invdec, sc 6. (57 sts)

Round 20: Sc 3, SW1, sc 2, SW2, sc 1, [invdec, sc 6] twice, invdec, sc 10, [invdec, sc 6] twice, invdec, sc 5. (51 sts)

Round 21: Sc 2, SW1, sc 3, invdec, SW2, sc 5, invdec, sc 6, invdec, sc 8, invdec, sc 5, invdec, sc 6, invdec, sc 4. (45 sts)

Round 22: Sc 1, SW1, sc 3, invdec, SW2, [sc 4, invdec] 6 times, sc 3. (38 sts)

Stuff the body, making sure to stuff the bottom and tummy a little more.

Stuff the arms by first inserting a tiny bit of stuffing into the doll's hands, insert the wire frame then continue stuffing the hands and arms lightly making sure to only stuff the top of the arms very lightly!

Round 23: Sc 2, SW1, sc 1, invdec, SW2, [sc 3, invdec] 6 times, sc 3. (31 sts)

Round 24: Sc 1, SW1, sc 1, invdec, sc 1, SW2, sc 1, invdec, [sc 2, invdec] 5 times, sc 3. (24 sts)

Round 25: SW1, [sc 1, invdec] twice, SW2, [sc 1, invdec] 6 times. (16 sts)

Stuff the body some more, especially the shoulders.

Round 26: SW1, [sc 2, invdec] twice, SW2, [sc 2, invdec] twice. (12 sts)

Round 27: SW1, sc 7, SW2, sc 5.

Round 28: Sc 1, SW1, sc 5, SW2, sc 6.

Round 29: Sc 2, SW1, sc 3, SW2, sc 7.

HEAD

Continue working in the round.

Round 1: [Sc 2 in next st, sc 2] 4 times. (16 sts)

Round 2: [Sc 2 in next st, sc 1] 8 times. (24 sts)

Round 3: [Sc 2 in next st, sc 2] 8 times. (32 sts)

Round 4: [Sc 2 in next st, sc 3] 8 times. (40 sts)

Round 5: [Sc 2 in next st, sc 4] 8 times. (48 sts)

Round 6: [Sc 2 in next st, sc 5] 8 times. (56 sts)

Round 7: Sc 56.

Round 8: Sc 9, SW1, sc 4, SW2, sc 43.

Round 9: Sc 8, SW1, sc 6, SW2, sc 42.

Rounds 10 and 11: Sc 7, SW1, sc 8, SW2, sc 41.

Round 12: Sc 8, SW1 sc 6, SW2 sc 42.

Round 13: Sc 9, SW1 sc 4, SW2 sc 43.

Round 14: [Sc 2, invdec] twice, SW1, [sc 2, invdec] twice, SW2, [sc 2, invdec] twice, sc 32. (50 sts)

Round 15: Sc 7, SW1, sc 5, SW2, sc 38.

Round 16: Sc 8, SW1, sc 3, SW2, sc 39.

Rounds 17 to 21: Sc 50.

Remove hook from working st and replace with a removable stitch marker to prevent your sts unravelling whilst you work the face as follows:

1. Embroider the nose in the middle of your doll's face over 2 sts between Rounds 12 and 13 (see General Techniques: Embroidery Stitches).

2. Mark out the placement of the eyes; they will be between Rounds 14 and 15 (2 rounds above the nose); there are 9 sts between the eyes.

3. For sclera and eye lashes (optional), embroider the sclera with white thread going around the lower half of the eye. After you insert the eyes, they will partially cover the sclera.

4. For the eye lashes, use embroidery yarn and make two lines on the outer edge of the eyes over 2 sts, one vertically and one diagonally (see Basic Doll).

5. For the eye brows, embroider a line over 4 sts, 4 rounds above the eyes slanting down 1 round; the eye brows are 8 sts apart.

6. Attach your safety eyes now (see General Techniques: Attaching Toy Safety Eyes).

Your doll is going to look a little wonky at this point, but don't worry, everything will straighten out as soon as you start stuffing the head.

Replace hook into working st.

Round 22: [Invdec, sc 23] twice. (48 sts)

Round 23: [Sc 4, invdec] 8 times. (40 sts)

Stuff the head very firmly, really take your time shaping the head properly while stuffing.

Round 24: [Sc 3, invdec] 8 times. (32 sts)

Round 25: [Sc 2, invdec] 8 times. (24 sts)

Round 26: [Sc 1, invdec] 8 times. (16 sts)

Round 27: [Invdec] 8 times. (8 sts)

Fasten off, weave in ends (see General Techniques: Weaving in Ends) and close all gaps.

Make sure you stuff the jaw and cheeks really well and press the eye area inwards while shaping. Don't forget to make the forehead and top of the doll's head nice and round.

EARS

We'll make a right and a left ear:

Using 2mm (US B/1) hook and skin tone of your choice, make a magic ring.

Left ear: [Ch 2, dc 1, hdc 5, ch 1, slst] into ring.

Using 2mm (US B/1) hook and skin tone of your choice, make a magic ring.

Right ear: [Ch 1, hdc 5, dc 1, ch 2, slst] into ring.

Sew the ears onto the side of your doll's head tightly, 6 sts away from the eyes. The top of the ear is on Round 15.

Use some blush to colour your doll's cheeks and paint on some freckles with safe acrylic paint if you like.

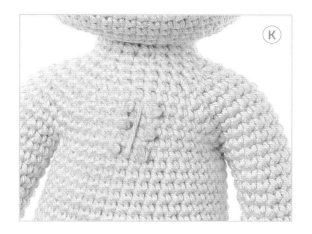

Scars

To add scars to your doll, mark where you'd like the scar to be, then embroider the scar using backstitch. Finish with bullion stitches on either side of the scar, about 2 sts apart (see General Techniques: Embroidery Stitches).

Your dolls are going to love their warrior scars.

Hair

Please don't be afraid to experiment with your doll's hair. You can personalise it to match the doll's recipient or make it all your own by choosing fun colours or even making different coloured hair strands.

We will crochet a wig cap first, then we'll crochet hair strands into the wig cap. You'll be able to decide how long and full you'd like your wig to be depending on how many stitches your chains are and how many slst you make into your cap between the strands.

Hair wig cap

A — For the hair we'll make a cap first, then we'll crochet our strands onto the cap.

Using 2.5mm (US C/2) hook and hair colour of your choice, make a magic ring.

The entire cap (up to Round 10) is crocheted in BLO.

Round 1 (RS): BLO: Sc 6 into ring. (6 sts)

Round 2: BLO: [Sc 2 in next st] 6 times. (12 sts)

Round 3: BLO: [Sc 1, sc 2 in next st] 6 times. (18 sts)

Round 4: BLO: [Sc 2, sc 2 in next st] 6 times. (24 sts)

Round 5: BLO: [Sc 3, sc 2 in next st] 6 times. (30 sts)

Round 6: BLO: [Sc 4, sc 2 in next st] 6 times. (36 sts)

Round 7: BLO: [Sc 5, sc 2 in next st] 6 times. (42 sts)

Round 8: BLO: [Sc 6, sc 2 in next st] 6 times. (48 sts)

Rounds 9 and 10: BLO: Sc 48.

Now we'll make the bottom back of the wig cap, working into FLO or BLO as instructed.

Round 11: FLO: Turn, ch 1 (does not count as st throughout), sc 17, turn.

Round 12: BLO: Ch 1, sc 17.

Fasten off and weave in ends (see General Techniques: Weaving in Ends).

Now we'll make the front of the cap.

Skip 4 sts of Round 10 and reconnect your yarn.

Round 13: BLO: Ch 1, sc 23, turn. (23 sts)

Round 14: FLO: Ch 1, sc 23, turn.

Round 15: BLO: Ch 1, sc2tog, sc 19, sc2tog. (21 sts)

Fasten off, leaving a long tail for sewing onto the doll's head.

B —
C —
D — Place the middle of the front flap of the cap on Round 22 of your doll's head and ease the cap onto the head so it fits snugly. Sew in place with small sts. The 2 gaps are for your doll's ears and the back of the cap will sit nicely on Round 7 of the head.

A

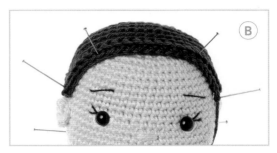

B

C

D

Hair strands

We'll start making the hair strands now. It's up to you to make them as long or short, curly or straight as you want. We will work into the spare loops from FLO and BLO sts of the wig cap. If you want the hair to be very thick, slst over 4 sts until the next strand, if you want less strands you can slst into more sts.

From Round 11 of your wig cap you should not slst more than 4–5 sts so that the front of your wig will look nice and full. Make sure to crochet hair strands until the very last round of the cap, working into the spare loops the entire time.

Making the hair takes time but it is really worth the effort!

(E) To make the hair strands; begin by connecting your yarn to the spare loop of st 1 in your cap.

WAVY HAIR

(F)
(G) Make your desired amount of ch sts, plus 1 ch, starting in second ch from hook, sc back in each ch until you reach the cap, slst into 8 sts of spare loops of cap.

Create the next strand in the same way.

STRAIGHT HAIR

(H) Make the strands like the wavy hair but straighten them carefully with a flat iron after you're done.

CURLY HAIR

Make your desired amount of ch sts plus 1 ch, starting in second ch from hook, work 2 sc in each ch until you reach your cap, slst into 3 sts of spare loops of cap.

Create the next strand in the same way.

The longer the chain, the longer your doll's hair will be and the fewer slst between strands will give your doll a fuller head of hair.

Getting dressed

Now it's time to make some clothes and shoes for your dolls. From t-shirts and trousers to skirts and dresses, you can create cool outfits in your favourite colours, before adding all the essential equipment you need to make your dolls unique and special.

Underpants

Materials

- 2mm (US B/1) crochet hook
- Approximately 10g (⅜oz) of Scheepjes Catona, or similar 4-ply (fingering weight) yarn, in your chosen colour
- Removable stitch markers or scrap yarn

Instructions

Make first pant leg as follows;

Using 2mm (US B/1) hook and chosen colour, ch 21.

(A) Slst in first ch to form a circle, being careful not to twist your ch sts.

Round 1 (RS): Ch 1, sc 1 in same ch as slst, sc 1 in each remaining ch, slst in first sc. (21 sts)

Fasten off and set aside.

Make second pant leg in the same way, but do not fasten off.

(B) You will now attach both pant legs by sc 1 in first st of first pant leg, sc 20 more around this pant leg, then sc 21 around second pant leg. (42 sts)

> *You can close up any holes later, using your yarn tail.*

Place marker.

Round 2: [Sc 7, sc 2 in next st] 5 times, sc 2. (47 sts)

Rounds 3 to 8: Sc 47.

Round 9: BLO: Hdc 47.

Fasten off.

FINISHING

Weave in ends (see General Techniques: Weaving in Ends) and close the small gap between pant legs using yarn tail (see General Techniques: Sewing Joins).

Skirt

Materials

- 2mm (US B/1) crochet hook
- Approximately 20g (¾oz) of Scheepjes Catona, or similar 4-ply (fingering weight) yarn, in your chosen colour
- 1 small button and regular sewing needle and thread (optional)

Instructions

The skirt is made in rows, crocheting back and forth, until Row 3, then it is worked in the round.

Using 2mm (US B/1) hook and chosen colour, ch 41.

If you'd like to add a button loop, just add 4 sts to your beginning ch and skip those extra sts along with the last st of your ch in Row 1 (so you would ch 44 and start in the seventh ch from the hook in Row 1).

(A) **Row 1:** Starting in third ch from hook, hdc 39, turn. (39 sts plus button loop)

Row 2: Ch 2 (does not count as st throughout), hdc 39 (leave the little loop untouched), turn.

Row 3: BLO: Ch 2, [hdc 2 in next st] to end of round **(do not turn)**. (78 sts)

(B) Slst into first st to form a circle, ch 1 (does not count as st) and start working in the round.

Rounds 4 to 11: Sc 78.

Make the scalloped edge as follows;

Round 12: BLO: [Skip 1 st, hdc 5 in next st, skip 1 st, slst in next st] 19 times, skip 1 st, hdc 5 in next st. (20 scallops)

Fasten off.

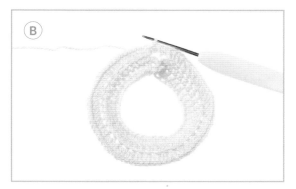

FINISHING

Weave in ends (see General Techniques: Weaving in Ends). Sew on a little button on to the back of your skirt (see General Techniques: Sewing on Buttons).

If you did not make the button loop you can completely close up the back or tie it with a piece of yarn.

Shorts

Materials

- 2.25mm (US C/2) crochet hook
- Approximately 15g (⁹⁄₁₆oz) of Scheepjes Catona, or similar 4-ply (fingering weight) yarn, in your chosen colour
- Removable stitch marker or scrap yarn

Instructions

Using 2.25mm (US C/2) hook and chosen colour, ch 23.

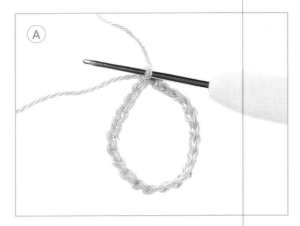

Slst into first ch to form a circle, being careful not to twist your ch sts.

Round 1: Ch 1 (does not count as st), hdc 1 in same ch as slst, hdc 1 in each remaining ch. (23 sts)

Round 2: BLO: Sc 23.

Rounds 3 to 5: Sc 23.

Slst in next st, fasten off and set aside.

Make second shorts leg in the same way, but do not fasten off.

You will now attach both shorts legs by sc 1 in first st of first shorts leg, sc 22 more around this shorts leg, then sc 23 around second shorts leg. (46 sts)

Place marker.

Round 6: [Sc 10, sc 2 in next st] 4 times, sc 2. (50 sts)

Rounds 7 to 13: Sc 50.

Round 14: BLO: Hdc 10, hdc invdec, hdc 13, hdc invdec, hdc 10, hdc invdec, hdc 9, hdc invdec. (46 sts)

Fasten off.

FINISHING

Weave in ends (see General Techniques: Weaving in Ends) and close the small gap between shorts legs (see General Techniques: Sewing Joins).

Trousers

Materials

- 2.25mm (US C/2) crochet hook
- Approximately 25g (⅞oz) of Scheepjes Catona, or similar 4-ply (fingering weight) yarn, in your chosen colour
- Removable stitch marker or scrap yarn
- 1 small button and regular sewing needle and thread

Instructions

Make first trouser leg as given for shorts, working to the end of Round 5, then continue as follows;

Rounds 6 to 22: Sc 23.

Slst in next st, fasten off and set aside.

Make second trouser leg in the same way, but do not fasten off.

(A) You will now attach both trouser legs by sc 1 in first st of first trouser leg, sc 22 more around this trouser leg, then sc 23 around second trouser leg. (46 sts)

Place marker.

Round 23: [Sc 10, sc 2 in next st] 4 times, sc 2. (50 sts)

Rounds 24 to 39: Sc 50

Round 30: BLO: Dc 50.

Slst in next st and fasten off.

FINISHING

Weave in ends (see General Techniques: Weaving in Ends) and close the small gap between trouser legs (see General Techniques: Sewing Joins).

Sew a little button on the front of your trousers (see General Techniques: Sewing on Buttons).

T-shirt

Materials

- 2.5mm (US C/2) crochet hook
- Approximately 25g (⅞oz) of Scheepjes Catona, or similar 4-ply (fingering weight) yarn, in your chosen colour
- Removable stitch markers or scrap yarn
- 1 small button and regular sewing needle and thread (optional)

Instructions

The t-shirt is made crocheting back and forth in rows; **ch 1 and turn** on each row.

Using 2.5mm (US C/2) hook and chosen colour, ch 25.

If you'd like to make a button loop, just add 4 sts to your beginning ch and skip those extra sts along with the last st of your ch in Row 1 (so you would ch 29 and start in the sixth ch from the hook in Row 1).

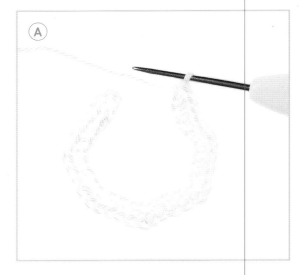

Ⓐ **Row 1:** Starting in second ch from hook, [sc 3, sc 2 in next ch] 6 times, turn. (30 sts plus button loop)

Row 2: FLO: Ch 1 (does not count as st throughout), [sc 3, sc 2 in next st] 7 times, sc 2, turn. (37 sts)

Leave the little loop untouched.

Row 3: Ch 1, sc 37, turn.

Row 4: Ch 1, [sc 5, sc 2 in next st] 6 times, sc 1, turn. (43 sts)

Row 5: Ch 1, [sc 7, sc 2 in next st] 5 times, sc 3, turn. (48 sts)

Row 6: Ch 1, [sc 11, sc 2 in next st] 4 times, turn. (52 sts)

Row 7: Ch 1, sc 7, ch 5, skip 11 sts, sc 16, ch 5, skip 11 sts, sc 7, turn. (30 sts plus 2 x ch 5 sps)

Row 8: Ch 1, sc 7, sc 6 into ch sp, sc 2 in next st, sc 14, sc 2 in next st, sc 6 into ch sp, sc 7, turn. (44 sts)

Row 9: Ch 1, sc 5, sc 2 in next st, sc 7, sc 2 in next st, sc 16, sc 2 in next st, sc 7, sc 2 in next st, sc 5, turn. (48 sts)

Rows 10 to 15: Ch 1, sc 48 turn.

Row 16: FLO: Ch 1, hdc 48.

(B) Fasten off.

FINISHING

Weave in ends (see General Techniques: Weaving in Ends) then sew up the back until Row 10 (see General Techniques: Sewing Joins).

Sew on a little button at the top of your t-shirt (see General Techniques: Sewing on Buttons).

(C) *If you did not make the button you can completely close up the back or tie it with a piece of yarn.*

For a striped t-shirt, switch colours every 2 rows, but don't cut your yarn between colour switches, simply leave the yarn and bring it up when you need it.

Sundress

Materials

- 2.25mm (US C/2) crochet hook
- Approximately 30g (1⅛oz) of Scheepjes Catona, or similar 4-ply (fingering weight) yarn, in your chosen colour, plus oddments of contrast colour for collar
- 1 small button and regular sewing needle and thread (optional)

Instructions

The first part of the dress is worked in rows, crocheting back and forth, to Row 11; **ch 1 and turn** on each row.

Using 2.25mm (US C/2) hook and chosen colour, work as given for t-shirt to end of Row 9. (48 sts)

Row 10: Ch 1, sc 48, turn.

(A) — **Row 11:** BLO: Ch 1, [2 hdc in next st] to end **(do not turn)**. (96 sts)

(B) — Slst into first st to form a circle, ch 1 (does not count as st) and start working in the round, starting in same st as slst.

Round 12: [2 hdc in next st, hdc 5] 16 times. (112 sts)

Rounds 13 to 23: Hdc 112.

Fasten off and weave in ends (see General Techniques: Weaving in Ends).

(A)

(B)

(C)

(D)

POCKETS (MAKE 2)

The pockets are worked in rows, crocheting back and forth, **ch 1 and turn** on each row.

Using 2.25mm (US C/2) hook and chosen colour, ch 9.

Row 1: Starting in second ch from hook, sc 8, turn. (8 sts)

Rows 2 to 6: Ch 1 (does not count as st throughout), sc 8, turn.

Row 7: Ch 1, sc2tog, sc 4, sc2tog. (6 sts)

C — Fasten off and leave a long tail for sewing onto dress.

> *The rounded edge is the bottom of the pocket.*

COLLAR (OPTIONAL)

The collar is worked in rows, crocheting back and forth, **ch 1 and turn** on each row.

D — Join chosen colour of yarn with a slst to the spare loop of first ch of Row 1.

Row 1: BLO: Ch 1 (does not count as st throughout), [sc 2, sc 2 in next st] 3 times, sc 2, slst 2, sc 2, [sc 2 in next st, sc 2] 3 times, turn. (30 sts)

Row 2: Ch 1, sc 3, hdc 2, dc 7, hdc 1, sc 1, slst 2, sc 1, hdc 1, dc 7, hdc 2, sc 3. (30 sts)

Fasten off and weave in ends (see General Techniques: Weaving in Ends).

FINISHING

Sew on a little button at the top of your dress (see General Techniques: Sewing on Buttons).

If you did not make the button you can completely close up the back or tie it with a piece of yarn.

Sew the pockets onto the front of your sundress, placing the top edge along Round 14 and leaving a gap of around 20 sts between the pockets (see General Techniques: Sewing Joins).

This collar will also work on all of the T-shirts!

Pinafore

Materials

- 2.5mm (US C/2) crochet hook
- Approximately 30g (1⅛oz) of Scheepjes Catona, or similar 4-ply (fingering weight) yarn, in your chosen colour
- Removable stitch markers or scrap yarn
- 1 small button and regular sewing needle and thread (optional)

Instructions

We'll start with the waistband to make the skirt and then add the bib.

Using 2.5mm (US C/2) hook, ch 50.

Slst in first ch to form a circle, being careful not to twist your ch sts.

Round 1: Ch 1 (does not count as st), hdc 50, slst in first st to close.

Round 2: BLO: [Sc 3, sc 2 in next st] 12 times, sc 2. (62 sts)

Rounds 3 to 16: Sc 62.

Round 17: Reverse sc 62 (see General Techniques: Reverse sc).

Fasten off.

BIB

The bib is worked in rows, crocheting back and forth, **ch 1 and turn** on each row.

Join yarn to back loop of st 19.

Row 1: Ch 1 (does not count as st throughout), sc 14, turn.

Rows 2 to 8: Ch 1, sc 14, turn.

Row 9: Ch 1, sc2tog, sc 10, sc2tog, turn. (12 sts)

Row 10: Ch 1, sc2tog, sc 8, sc2tog, turn. (10 sts)

Fasten off.

BACK AND STRAPS

This part of your pinafore is worked in rows, crocheting back and forth, **ch 1 and turn** on each row.

Join yarn to BLO of st 45. Place marker.

Row 1: BLO: Ch 1 (does not count as st throughout), sc 12, turn.

Rows 2 to 4: Ch 1, sc 12, turn.

Row 5: Ch 1, sc2tog, sc 8, sc2tog, turn. (10 sts)

Row 6: Ch 1, sc2tog, sc 6, sc2tog, turn. (8 sts)

Row 7: Ch 1, sc2tog, sc 4, sc2tog, turn. (6 sts)

Row 8: Ch 1, sc2tog, sc 2, sc2tog, turn. (4 sts)

(E)(F) **Row 9:** Ch 20, starting in fourth ch from hook, sc 17, sc 3 in back of ch, ch 20, starting in fourth ch from hook, sc 17, slst in last st of dress.

Fasten off, weave in all ends (see General Techniques: Weaving in Ends).

Sew two little buttons onto the front patch and close (see General Techniques: Sewing on Buttons).

POCKET

The pocket is worked in rows, crocheting back and forth, **ch 1 and turn** on each row.

Ch 9.

Row 1: Starting in second ch from hook, sc 8. (8 sts)

Rows 2 to 5: Ch 1 (does not count as st throughout), sc 8, turn.

Row 6: Ch 1, sc2tog, sc 4, sc2tog, turn. (6 sts)

Fasten off, leaving a long thread, and sew onto the front of the bib (see General Techniques: Sewing Joins). The rounded edge will be the bottom of the pocket, place it on Row 2 of the bib. Weave in ends (see General Techniques: Weaving in Ends).

(E)

(F)

Overalls/dungarees

Materials

- 2.25mm (US C/2) crochet hook
- Approximately 30g (1⅛oz) of Scheepjes Catona Denim, or similar 4-ply (fingering weight) yarn, in your chosen colour
- Removable stitch markers or scrap yarn
- 2 small buttons and regular sewing needle and thread

Instructions

Follow the trousers pattern through to Round 30. (50 sts)

Slst in next st, fasten off and weave in ends (see General Techniques: Weaving in Ends).

The next part of your overalls/dungarees is worked in rows, crocheting back and forth, **ch 1 and turn** on each row.

Ⓐ With right side facing, join yarn with a slst to BLO of st 19.

Row 1: BLO: Ch 1 (does not count as st throughout), sc 1 in same st, sc 13, turn. (14 sts)

Rows 2 to 9: Ch 1, sc 14, turn.

Ⓑ **Row 10:** Ch 1, sc2tog, sc 10, sc2tog, turn. (12 sts)

Fasten off.

BACK AND STRAPS

This part of your overalls/dungarees is worked in rows, crocheting back and forth, **ch 1 and turn** on each row.

(C)— Join yarn to BLO of st 44.

Place marker.

Row 1: BLO: Ch 1, sc 12, turn. (12 sts)

Rows 2 to 5: Ch 1 (does not count as st throughout), sc 12, turn.

Row 6: Ch 1, sc2tog, sc 8, sc2tog, turn. (10 sts)

Row 7: Ch 1, sc2tog, sc 6, sc2tog, turn. (8 sts)

Row 8: Ch 1, sc2tog, sc 4, sc2tog, turn. (6 sts)

(D)— **Row 9:** Ch 21, starting in fifth ch from hook, hdc 17, sc 5 along back of overalls/dungarees, ch 21, skip 4 ch, hdc 17, slst into last st on back of overalls/dungarees.

Fasten off and weave in all ends (see General Techniques: Weaving in Ends).

Sew two little buttons onto the front patch (see General Techniques: Sewing on Buttons), cross over the straps in the back and close.

You could make your pocket in a contrast colour to make it stand out.

POCKET

The pocket is worked in rows, crocheting back and forth, **ch 1 and turn** on each row.

Using 2.25mm (US C/2) crochet hook, ch 9.

Row 1: Starting in second ch from hook, sc 8 in ch, turn. (8 sts)

Rows 2 to 4: Ch 1 (does not count as st throughout), sc 8, turn.

Row 5: Ch 1, sc2tog, sc 4, sc2tog. (6 sts)

Fasten off, leaving a long thread.

FINISHING

Weave in ends (see General Techniques: Weaving in Ends). Sew pockets onto the front of your trousers, lining up the bottom of the pocket with Round 2 of the trousers (see General Techniques: Sewing Joins).

The rounded edge is the bottom of the pocket.

Short overalls/dungarees

Follow the shorts pattern through to Round 13 then go to Round 30 of the trousers pattern and continue with the overalls/dungarees pattern until the end.

> *You can use lots of different colours for the overalls and can even make them striped.*

You can adapt the length of your doll's clothes to fit their limb loss.

Baggy trousers

Materials

- 2.5mm (US C/2) crochet hook
- Approximately 25g (⅞oz) of Scheepjes Catona, or similar 4-ply (fingering weight) yarn, in your chosen colour
- Removable stitch markers or scrap yarn
- 1 small button and regular sewing needle and thread

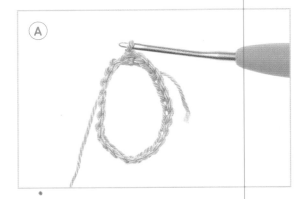

Instructions

Make first trouser leg as follows;

Using 2.5mm (US C/2) hook and chosen colour, ch 24.

(A) Slst in first ch to form a circle, being careful not to twist your ch sts.

Round 1: Ch 1 (does not count as st), hdc 1 in same st as slst, hdc 1 in each remaining ch. (24 sts)

(B) **Round 2:** BLO: [Sc 2 in next st, sc 1] 12 times. (36 sts)

Rounds 3 to 24: Sc 36.

Slst in next st, fasten off and set aside.

Make second trouser leg in the same way but do not fasten off.

(C) You will attach both trouser legs now by sc 1 in first st of first trouser leg, sc 35 more around this trouser leg, then sc 36 around second trouser leg. (72 sts)

Place marker.

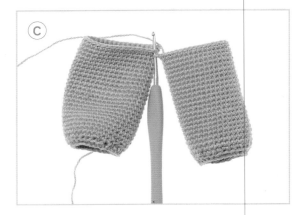

Rounds 25 to 30: Sc 72.

Round 31: [Sc 4, invdec] 12 times. (60 sts)

Round 32: [Sc 3, invdec) 12 times. (48 sts)

Round 33: Sc 48.

Round 34: BLO: Hdc 48.

Fasten off.

FINISHING

Weave in ends (see General Techniques: Weaving in Ends).

Sew a little button on the front of your trousers (see General Techniques: Sewing on Buttons).

Baggy overalls/dungarees

Materials

- 2.5mm (US C/2) crochet hook
- Approximately 30g (1⅛oz) of Scheepjes Catona, or similar 4-ply (fingering weight) yarn, in your chosen colour
- Removable stitch markers or scrap yarn
- 2 small buttons and regular sewing needle and thread

Instructions

Follow the baggy trousers pattern through to Round 34.

The next part of your overalls/dungarees is worked in rows, crocheting back and forth, **ch 1 and turn** on each row.

(A) Join your yarn with a slst to BLO of st 17.

Row 1: BLO: Ch 1 (does not count as st throughout), sc 1 in same st as slst, sc 18, turn. (19 sts)

Rows 2 to 9: Ch 1, sc 19, turn.

Row 10: Ch 1, sc2tog, sc 15, sc2tog, turn. (17 sts)

Row 11: Ch 1, sc2tog, sc 13, sc2tog. (15 sts)

(B) Fasten off.

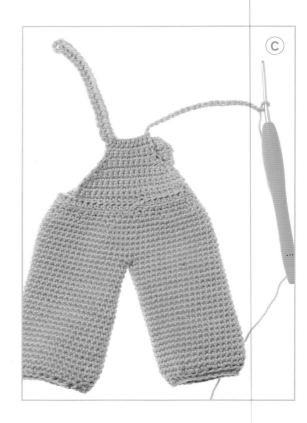

BACK AND STRAPS

This part of your overalls/dungarees is worked in rows, crocheting back and forth, **ch 1 and turn** on each row.

Join yarn with a slst to BLO of st 40.

Place marker.

Row 1: BLO: Ch 1 (does not count as st throughout), sc 1 in same st as slst, sc 18, turn. (19 sts)

Rows 2 to 4: Ch 1, sc 19.

Row 5: Ch 1, sc2tog, sc 15, sc2tog, turn. (17 sts)

Row 6: Ch 1, sc2tog, sc 13, sc2tog, turn. (15 sts)

Row 7: Ch 1, sc2tog, sc 11, sc2tog, turn. (13 sts)

Row 8: Ch 1, sc2tog, sc 9, sc2tog, turn. (11 sts)

Row 9: Ch 1, sc2tog, sc 7, sc2tog, turn. (9 sts)

Rows 10 and 11: Ch 1, sc 9.

Row 12: Ch 22, starting in fourth ch from hook, hdc 19 along ch, sc 8 along back of overalls, ch 22, starting in fourth ch from hook, hdc 19 along ch, slst into last st on back of overalls.

Fasten off.

FINISHING

Weave in ends (see General Techniques: Weaving in Ends) and sew two little buttons onto the front patch and close (see General Techniques: Sewing on Buttons).

POCKET

The pocket is worked in rows, crocheting back and forth, **ch 1 and turn** on each row.

Ch 9.

Row 1: Starting in second ch from hook, sc 8 along ch, turn. (8 sts)

Rows 2 to 5: Ch 1 (does not count as st throughout), sc 8, turn.

Row 6: Ch 1, sc2tog, sc 4, sc2tog. (6 sts)

Fasten off, leaving a long thread and sew onto the front of your trousers, lining up the bottom of the pocket with Round 2 of the trousers (see General Techniques: Sewing Joins). Weave in ends (see General Techniques: Weaving in Ends).

The rounded edge will be the bottom of the pocket.

Cardigan

Materials

- 2.5mm (US C/2) crochet hook
- Approximately 40g (1½oz) of Scheepjes Catona, or similar 4-ply (fingering weight) yarn, in your chosen colour, plus oddments of contrast colour for collar (optional)
- Removable stitch markers or scrap yarn
- 1 small button and regular sewing needle and thread (optional)

You can make the cardigan in lots of different colours and colour combinations.

Instructions

The cardigan is made in rows, crocheting back and forth, **ch 1 and turn** on each row.

Using 2.5mm (US C/2) hook, ch 29.

Row 1: Starting in second ch from hook, [hdc 3, hdc 2 in next ch] 7 times, turn. (35 sts)

Row 2: FLO: Ch 1 (does not count as st throughout), [sc 3, sc 2 in next st] 8 times, sc 3, turn. (43 sts)

Row 3: Ch 1, sc 43, turn.

Row 4: Ch 1, [sc 5, sc 2 in next st] 7 times, sc 1, turn. (50 sts)

Row 5: Ch 1, [sc 7, sc 2 in next st] 6 times, sc 2, turn. (56 sts)

Row 6: Ch 1, [sc 13, sc 2 in next st] 4 times, turn. (60 sts)

Ⓐ **Row 7:** Ch 1, sc 10, ch 7, skip 12 sts, sc 16, ch 7, skip 12 sts, sc 10, turn. (36 sts + 14 ch)

Ⓑ **Row 8:** Ch 1, sc 10, sc 7 in ch, [sc 2 in next st, sc 2] 5 times, sc 2 in next st, sc 7 in ch, sc 10, turn. (56 sts)

Row 9: Ch 1, sc 9, sc 2 in next st, sc 36, sc 2 in next st, sc 9, turn. (58 sts)

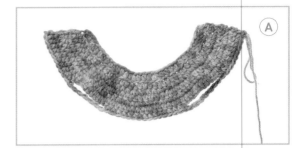

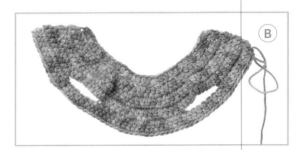

Rows 10 to 18: Ch 1, sc 58, turn.

Row 19: BLO: Ch 1, dc 58, turn.

(C) Fasten off and weave in ends (see General Techniques: Weaving in Ends).

SLEEVES

(D) Connect yarn to any st in the sleeve opening, ch 1 (does not count as st), sc 21 around.

Place marker. Continue working in the round.

Rounds 1 to 13: Sc 21.

Round 14: [Sc 2, invdec] 5 times, sc 1. (16 sts)

Round 15: BLO: Hdc 16.

(E) Repeat on other side for second sleeve.

FINISHING

Connect yarn to the bottom right corner of the cardigan.

(F) **Row 1:** Ch 2, hdc 3, [ch 1, skip 1 st, hdc 4] 4 times all the way up the front opening.

Fasten off. Connect yarn to the top left corner of the cardigan.

Row 1: Ch 2, hdc all the way down the front opening.

Fasten off and weave in ends (see General Techniques: Weaving in Ends).

Sew 4 little buttons on to the left side of the cardigan (see General Techniques: Sewing on Buttons).

ADDING A COLLAR (OPTIONAL)

The collar is worked in rows, crocheting back and forth, **ch 1 and turn** after each row.

Join yarn to the 29th ch of Row 1. Work into spare loops (BLO) of first row and start in same st.

Row 1: BLO: Ch 1 (does not count as st throughout), [sc 1, sc 2 in next st, sc 2, sc 2 in next st] 5 times, sc 1, sc 2 in next st, sc 1, turn. (39 sts)

Row 2: Ch 1, hdc 2 in first st, hdc 37, hdc 2 in last st, turn. (41 sts)

Fasten off and weave in ends (see General Techniques: Weaving in Ends).

Add a cute collar!

Coat

Materials

- 2.5mm (US C/2) crochet hook
- Approximately 60g (2⅛oz) of Scheepjes Catona, or similar 4-ply (fingering weight) yarn, in your chosen colours, plus oddments of contrast colour for collar
- Removable stitch markers or scrap yarn
- 1 small button and regular sewing needle and thread (optional)

You can make the coat using just one colour or with a cute striped pattern using three colours. I have written both options down for you.

Instructions

Colour changes are indicated with: SW1, SW2, or SW3.

Change the colour with the last st of the previous row. When you switch colours, don't cut your yarn, just carry it up to when you need it being careful not to pull the yarn tightly.

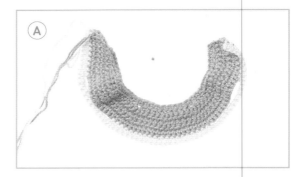

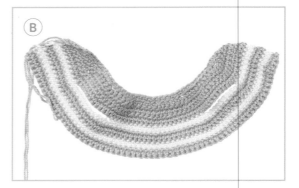

Option 1

STRIPED COAT

The coat is made in rows, crocheting back and forth, **ch 1 and turn** on each row.

Using 2.5mm (US C/2) hook and first colour, ch 33.

Row 1: Starting in second ch from hook, [sc 3, sc 2 in next st] 8 times, turn. (40 sts)

Row 2: FLO: Ch 1 (does not count as st throughout), [sc 4, sc 2 in next st] 8 times, turn. (48 sts)

Row 3: Ch 1, sc 48, turn.

Row 4: Ch 1, [sc 5, sc 2 in next st] 8 times, turn. (56 sts)

Row 5: SW2, ch 1, [sc 7, sc 2 in next st] 7 times, turn. (63 sts)

Row 6: Ch 1, sc 63, turn.

(A) **Row 7:** SW3, ch 1, sc 9, ch 10, skip 12 sts, sc 10, sc 2 in next st, sc 10, ch 10, skip 12 sts, sc 9, turn. (40 sts + 20 ch)

Row 8: Ch 1, sc 8, sc 2 in next st, sc 10 in ch, sc 2 in next st, sc 20, sc 2 in next st, sc 10 in ch, sc 2 in next st, sc 8, turn. (64 sts)

Row 9: SW2, ch 1, sc 9, sc 2 in next st, sc 10, sc 2 in next st, sc 22, sc 2 in next st, sc 10, sc 2 in next st, sc 9, turn. (68 sts)

Row 10: Ch 1, sc 32, [sc 2 in next st] 4 times, sc 32, turn. (72 sts)

Row 11: SW3, ch 1, sc 72, turn.

Row 12: Ch 1, sc 72, turn.

Row 13: SW2, ch 1, sc 72, turn.

(B) **Row 14:** Ch 1, sc 72, turn.

Rows 15 to 20: SW1, ch 1, sc 72, turn.

Row 21: SW2, ch 1, sc 72, turn.

Row 22: Ch 1 sc 72, turn.

Row 23: SW3, ch 1, sc 72, turn.

Row 24: Ch 1, sc 72, turn.

Row 25: SW2, ch 1, sc 72, turn.

Row 26: Ch 1, sc 72, turn.

Row 27: SW3, ch 1, sc 72, turn.

Row 28: Ch 1, sc 72, turn.

Row 29: SW2, ch 1, sc 72, turn.

Row 30: Ch 1, sc 72, turn.

Rows 31 and 32: SW1, ch 1, sc 72, turn.

(C) Fasten off and weave in ends (see General Techniques: Weaving in Ends).

SLEEVES

(D) Connect third colour to any st in the sleeve opening and sc 24 around.

Place marker. Continue working in the round.

Leave off the hood if desired.

Round 1: Sc 24.

Round 2: SW2, sc 24.

Round 3: Sc 24.

Round 4: SW3, sc 24.

Round 5: Sc 24.

Round 6: SW2, sc 24.

Round 7: Sc 24.

Rounds 8 to 15: SW1, sc 24.

Round 16: FLO: Sc 24.

Rounds 17 and 18: Hdc 24.

Fasten off and weave in ends (see General Techniques: Weaving in Ends).

Repeat on other side for second sleeve.

FINISHING THE FRONT

The front is worked in rows, crocheting back and forth, **ch 1 and turn** on each row.

Connect first colour to the bottom right corner:

Row 1: Ch 1 (does not count as st throughout), [hdc 7, ch 1, skip 1 st] 4 times all the way up the front opening, turn. (32 sts)

Row 2: Ch 1, sc 32.

Fasten off.

Connect first colour to the top left corner:

Row 1: Ch 1, sc 32 all the way down the front opening, turn.

Row 2: Ch 1, sc 32.

Fasten off and weave in all ends (see General Techniques: Weaving in Ends).

Sew 4 little buttons onto the left side of the coat (see General Techniques: Sewing on Buttons).

HOOD (OPTIONAL)

The hood is worked in rows, crocheting back and forth, **ch 1 and turn** on each row.

With the inside of the coat facing you, join first colour to the back loop of first sts on Round 1 of the coat.

Row 1: BLO: Ch 1 (does not count as st throughout), [sc 3, sc 2 in next st] 8 times, turn. (40 sts)

Row 2: Ch 1, [sc 3, sc 2 in next st] 10 times, turn. (50 sts)

Row 3: SW2, ch 1, sc 50, turn.

Row 4: Ch 1, sc 50, turn.

Row 5: SW3, ch 1, sc 50, turn.

Row 6: Ch 1, [sc 4, sc 2 in next st] 10 times, turn. (60 sts)

Row 7: SW2, ch 1, sc 60, turn.

Row 8: Ch 1, sc 60, turn.

Row 9: SW3, ch 1, sc 60, turn.

Row 10: Ch 1, sc 60, turn.

Row 11: SW2, ch 1, sc 60, turn.

Row 12: Ch 1, sc 60, turn.

Row 13: SW1, ch 1, sc 60, turn.

Rows 14 to 18: Ch 1, sc 60, turn.

Row 19: SW2, ch 1, sc 60, turn.

Row 20: Ch 1, sc 60, turn.

Row 21: SW3, ch 1, sc 60, turn.

Row 22: Ch 1, sc 60, turn.

Row 23: SW2, ch 1, sc 60, turn.

Row 24: Ch 1, sc 60, turn.

Row 25: SW3, ch 1, sc 60, turn.

Row 26: Ch 1, sc 60, turn.

Row 27: SW2, ch 1, sc 60, turn.

Row 28: Ch 1, sc 60, turn.

Row 29: SW1, ch 1, sc 60, turn.

Rows 30 to 34: Ch 1, sc 60, turn.

Row 35: SW2, ch 1, sc 60, turn.

Row 36: Ch 1, sc 60, turn.

Row 37: SW3, ch 1, sc 60 turn.

(I) **Row 38:** Ch 1, sc 60.

(J) Fold the top of the hood in half and sc 30 through both sides to close.

Connect first colour to the first sts of Row 1 of the hood and sc around the edge.

Fasten off and weave in ends (see General Techniques: Weaving in Ends).

Option 2

COAT WITHOUT COLOUR CHANGES

The coat is worked in rows, crocheting back and forth, **ch 1 and turn** on each row.

Using 2.5mm (US C/2) hook, ch 33.

Row 1: Starting in second ch from hook, [sc 3, sc 2 in next st] 8 times, turn. (40 sts)

Row 2: FLO: Ch 1 (does not count as st throughout), [sc 4, sc 2 in next st] 8 times, turn. (48 sts)

Row 3: Ch 1, sc 48, turn.

Row 4: Ch 1 [sc 5, sc 2 in next st] 8 times, turn. (56 sts)

Row 5: Ch 1, [sc 7, sc 2 in next st] 7 times, turn. (63 sts)

Row 6: Ch 1, sc 63, turn.

Row 7: Ch 1, sc 9, ch 10, skip 12 sts, sc 10, sc 2 in next st, sc 10, ch 10, skip 12 sts, sc 9, turn. (40 sts + 20 ch)

Row 8: Ch 1, sc 8, sc 2 in next st, sc 10 in ch, sc 2 in next st, sc 20, sc 2 in next st, sc 10 in ch, sc 2 in next st, sc 8, turn. (64 sts)

Row 9: Ch 1. sc 9, sc 2 in next st, sc 10, sc 2 in next st, sc 22, sc 2 in next st, sc 10, sc 2 in next st, sc 9, turn. (68 sts)

Row 10: Ch 1, sc 32, [sc 2 in next st] 4 times, sc 32, turn. (72 sts)

Rows 11 to 32: Ch 1, sc 72, turn.

Fasten off and weave in ends (see General Techniques: Weaving in Ends).

SLEEVES

Connect yarn to any st in the sleeve opening and sc 24 around.

Place marker. Continue working in the round

Rounds 1 to 15: Sc 24.

Round 16: FLO: Sc 24.

Rounds 17 and 18: Hdc 24.

Fasten off and weave in ends (see General Techniques: Weaving in Ends).

Repeat on other side for second sleeve.

FINISHING THE FRONT

The front is worked in rows, crocheting back and forth, **ch 1 and turn** on each row. Join yarn to the bottom right corner:

Row 1: Ch 1 (does not count as st throughout), [hdc 7, ch 1, skip 1 st] 4 times all up the front opening, turn.

Row 2: Ch 1, sc 32.

Fasten off.

Connect your yarn to the top left corner:

Rows 1 to 2: Ch 1, sc 32 all down the front opening.

Fasten off and weave in ends (see General Techniques: Weaving in Ends).

Sew 4 buttons onto the left side of the coat (see General Techniques: Sewing on Buttons).

Co-ordinate your coat and boots to create a matching outfit.

HOOD (OPTIONAL)

The hood is worked in rows, crocheting back and forth, **ch 1 and turn** on each row.

With the inside of the coat facing you, join the yarn to the back loop of first ch of the coat.

Row 1: BLO: Ch 1 (does not count as st throughout), [sc 3, sc 2 in next st] 8 times, turn. (40 sts)

Row 2: Ch 1, [sc 3, sc 2 in next st] 10 times, turn. (50 sts)

Rows 3 to 5: Ch 1, sc 50, turn.

Row 6: Ch 1, [sc 4, sc 2 in next st] 10 times, turn. (60 sts)

Rows 7 to 38: Ch 1, sc 60, turn.

Fold the top of the hood in half and sc 30 through both sides to close.

Join the yarn to the first sts of Row 1 of the hood and sc around the edge.

Fasten off and weave in ends (see General Techniques: Weaving in Ends).

You can make the hood bigger or smaller by adding or subtracting rows.

Finishing touches for both options (optional)

The collar, ears and pockets are all worked in rows, **ch 1 and turn** on each row.

COLLAR

With the top of the coat facing you, connect the yarn to the first front loop on round 2.

Row 1: Ch 1 (does not count as st throughout), [sc 2 in next st, sc 2] to end, turn. (52 sts)

Rows 2 to 4: Ch 1, sc 52, turn.

Fasten off and weave in ends (see General Techniques: Weaving in Ends).

KITTEN EARS (MAKE 2)

Using 2.5mm (US C/2) hook, make a magic ring.

Row 1: Ch 1 (does not count as st throughout), sc 3 into ring, turn.

Row 2: Ch 1, sc 2 in next st, sc 1, sc 2 in next st, turn. (5 sts)

Row 3: Ch 1, sc 2 in next st, sc 3, sc 2 in next st, turn. (7 sts)

Row 4: Ch 1, sc 2 in next st, sc 5, sc 2 in next st, turn. (9 sts)

Rows 5 to 8: Ch 1, sc 9, turn.

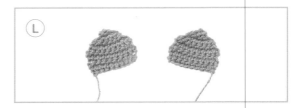

Fasten off, leaving a long tail. Sew the ears onto each side of the hood between Rounds 20 and 26 (see General Techniques: Sewing Joins).

POCKETS (MAKE 2)

Using 2.5mm (US C/2) hook, ch 9.

Row 1: Sc 1 in second ch from hook, sc 7, turn. (8 sts)

Rows 2 to 6: Ch 1 (does not count as st throughout), sc 8, turn.

Row 7: Ch 1, sc2tog, sc 4, sc2tog, turn. (6 sts)

Row 8: Ch 1, sc2tog, sc 2, sc2tog, turn. (4 sts)

Fasten off and leave a long tail. Finally, sew the pockets onto the coat (see General Techniques: Sewing Joins).

If you're making pockets for the striped coat, make sure you switch the colours on the pockets according to the colours on the coat.

Leg warmers

Materials

- 2.25mm (US C/2) crochet hook
- Scraps of Scheepjes Catona, or similar 4-ply (fingering weight) yarn, in your chosen colour or colours

You can make the leg warmers in one colour or make them extra cute by switching the colours every few rounds.

Instructions

Using 2.25mm (US C/2) hook, ch 18.

Slst in first ch to form a circle, being careful not to twist your ch sts.

Round 1: Ch 2 (does not count as st), hdc 18. (18 sts)

Round 2: BLO: [Hdc 2, hdc 2 in next st] 6 times. (24 sts)

Round 3: Hdc 24.

Round 4: BLO: Hdc 24.

Round 5: Hdc 24.

Round 6: BLO: Hdc 24.

Round 7: Hdc 24.

Round 8: BLO: Hdc 24.

Repeat the last 4 rounds once more.

Round 13: [Hdc 2, hdc invdec] 6 times. (18 sts)

Round 14: BLO: Hdc 18.

Fasten off and weave in ends (see General Techniques: Weaving in Ends).

Scarf

Materials

- 2.5mm (US C/2) crochet hook
- Scraps of Scheepjes Catona, or similar 4-ply (fingering weight) yarn, in your chosen colour

Instructions

The scarf is worked in rows, crocheting back and forth, **ch 1 and turn** on each row.

Using 2.5mm (US C/2) hook, ch 91.

Row 1: Sc 1 in second ch from hook, sc 89, turn. (90 sts)

Rows 2 to 5: Ch 1 (does count as st throughout), sc 90, turn.

Fasten off and weave in ends (see General Techniques: Weaving in Ends).

You can make a striped scarf as well, just switch colours for each new round.

Beanie

Materials

- 2.5mm (US C/2) crochet hook
- Approximately 40g (1½oz) in total of Scheepjes Catona, or similar 4-ply (fingering weight) yarn, in your chosen colours

Instructions

The pattern is worked in 2 colours, but you can make it in just one colour or completely colourful.

Colour changes are indicated with: SW1 or SW2.

Using 2.5mm (US C/2) hook and first colour, make a magic ring.

Round 1: Hdc 12 into ring.

Round 2: [Hdc 2 in next st] 12 times. (24 sts)

Round 3: [Hdc 2, hdc 2 in next st] 8 times. (32 sts)

Round 4: SW2, BLO: [Hdc 3, hdc 2 in next st] 8 times. (40 sts)

Round 5: [Hdc 4, hdc 2 in next st] 8 times. (48 sts)

Round 6: SW1, BLO: [Hdc 5, hdc 2 in next st] 8 times. (56 sts)

Round 7: [Hdc 6, hdc 2 in next st] 8 times. (64 sts)

Round 8: SW2, BLO: Hdc 64.

Round 9: Hdc 64.

Round 10: SW1, BLO: Hdc 64.

Round 11: Hdc 64.

Repeat last 4 rounds once more.

Round 16: SW2, BLO: Hdc 64.

Round 17: Hdc 64.

BORDER

Round 18: BLO: Dc 64.

Round 19: [Dc 1 around front post of st below, dc 1 around back post of st below] 32 times. (64 sts)

Fasten off and weave in ends (see General Techniques: Weaving in Ends).

If you're making the hat for a doll without hair, you can thread a piece of yarn through the back sts of Round 19 so you can tighten the hat around your doll's head.

Headband

Materials

- 2mm (US B/1) crochet hook
- Scraps of Scheepjes Catona, or similar 4-ply (fingering weight) yarn, in your chosen colour

Instructions

Using 2mm (US B/1) hook, ch 54.

Slst in first ch to form a circle, being careful not to twist your ch sts.

Round 1: Ch 2 (does not count as st), hdc 54, slst in first st to close.

Fasten off and weave in ends (see General Techniques: Weaving in Ends).

Every doll needs some cute accessories. Make them in lots of colours to match their outfits.

LITTLE BOWS (MAKE 3)

Using 2mm (US B/1) hook and chosen colour, ch 3, dc 2 in first ch, ch 3, slst in first st of ch.

Repeat for the second half of bow.

Wrap the yarn around the middle of the bow a few times, fasten off and weave in ends (see General Techniques: Weaving in Ends).

Sew the bows onto your headband.

Purse

Materials

- 2.25mm (US C/2) crochet hook
- Approximately 15g (9/16oz) of Scheepjes Catona, or similar 4-ply (fingering weight) yarn, in your chosen colour

Instructions

Using 2.25mm (US C/2) hook, make a magic ring.

Round 1: Sc 6 into ring.

Round 2: [Sc 2 in next st] 6 times. (12 sts)

Round 3: [Sc 1, sc 2 in next st] 6 times. (18 sts)

Round 4: [Sc 2, sc 2 in next st] 6 times. (24 sts)

Round 5: [Sc 3, sc 2 in next st] 6 times. (30 sts)

Fasten off and weave in ends (see General Techniques: Weaving in Ends).

(A) Make another circle just the same.

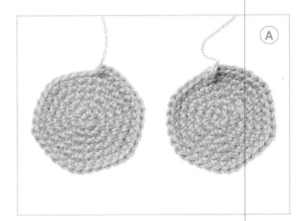

CONNECTION STRAP

Using 2.25mm (US C/2) hook, ch 34.

Round 1: Staring in third st of ch, hdc 32. (32 sts)

Fasten off and weave in ends (see General Techniques: Weaving in Ends).

Now we'll connect both circles to the strap:

(B) Hold the wrong side of the strap and wrong side of one circle together and slst along 34 sts to connect them (see General Techniques: Slip Stitch Seam).

Now take the second circle and connect it to the other side of the strap the same way.

(C) Fasten off and weave in ends (see General Techniques: Weaving in Ends).

LITTLE EARS

Ⓓ Join yarn to the first connection slst, (hdc 1, dc 5, hdc 1, slst) in same st.

Fasten off and weave in ends (see General Techniques: Weaving in Ends).

Ⓔ Repeat in the last connection slst for the second ear.

STRAP AND DECORATION

Ch 47.

Sew ends on either side of the purse to make a strap.

Embroider some whiskers onto the purse (see General Techniques: Embroidery Stitches).

LITTLE BOW (OPTIONAL)

Using 2mm (US B/1) hook and chosen colour, ch 3, dc 2 in first ch, ch 3, slst in first st of ch.

Repeat for the second half of bow.

Wrap the yarn around the middle of the bow a few times, fasten off and weave in ends (see General Techniques: Weaving in Ends).

Sew the bow onto the front of your purse.

Boots

Materials

- 2mm (US B/1) crochet hook
- Approximately 10g (⅜oz) of Scheepjes Catona, or similar 4-ply (fingering weight) yarn, in your chosen colour(s) for each pair
- Removable stitch markers or scrap yarn
- Hard cardboard or plastic for shoe inners (optional)

Instructions

SOLES (MAKE 2)

You can make the bottom and top sole in two different colours to make your boots extra cool!

Using 2mm (US B/1) hook and chosen colour, ch 6.

Round 1 (RS): Sc 1 in second ch from hook, sc 3, sc 3 in next ch, sc 4 along opposite side of ch. (11 sts)

Place marker.

Round 2: Sc 3 in first st, sc 1, hdc 1, dc 1, dc 2 in next st, dc 3 in next st (this is the top st of your sole), dc 2 in next st, dc 1, hdc 1, sc 2. (17 sts)

Round 3: Sc 2 in next st, sc 3 in next st, sc 2 in next st, sc 4, [2 hdc in next st] 6 times, sc 4. (27 sts)

Round 4: Sc 1, sc 2 in next st, sc 3 in next st, sc 2 in next st, sc 8, [sc 2 in next st] 8 times, sc 7. (39 sts)

Round 5: Sc 5, slst in next st, stop the round here.

Fasten off and weave in ends (see General Techniques: Weaving in Ends). Make another sole in the same way.

(A)—Crochet both soles together by holding them wrong sides together and slst through both of the soles (see General Techniques: Slip Stitch Seam).

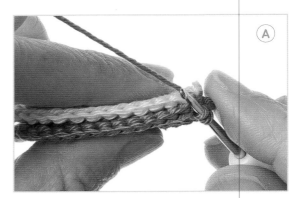

(B) Now connect your yarn to the back loop of first slst in the back of the soles to continue working on your boot.

Place marker.

Round 1: Ch 1, sc 39.

(C) Round 2: Hdc 12, [dc2tog] 8 times, hdc 11. (31 sts)

Round 3: Hdc 12, dc2tog, dc3tog, dc2tog, hdc 12. (27 sts)

Round 4: Sc 12, dc3tog, sc 10, invdec. (24 sts)

Round 5: Hdc 11, dc3tog, hdc 10. (22 sts)

Rounds 6 to 8: Hdc 22.

Round 9: BLO: Sc 22.

Fasten off and weave in ends (see General Techniques: Weaving in Ends).

Make the laces with a piece of yarn (optional).

> *You can insert a piece of cardboard or hard plastic between the two soles to make your boots sturdier.*

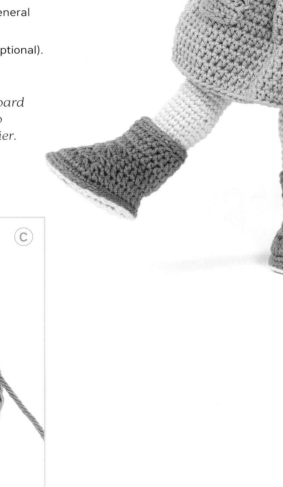

(C)

Trainers

Materials

- 2mm (US B/1) crochet hook
- Approximately 10g (⅜oz) of Scheepjes Catona, or similar 4-ply (fingering weight) yarn, in your chosen colour(s) for each pair
- Removable stitch markers or scrap yarn
- Hard cardboard or plastic for shoe inners (optional)

Instructions

Follow the instructions for Boots through to Round 4 of top of boots.

Round 5: Slst 11, hdc BLO 1, hdc BLO 3 in next st, hdc BLO 1, slst 10. (26 sts)

Fasten off and weave in ends (see General Techniques: Weaving in Ends).

Make the laces with a piece of yarn.

Sandals

Materials

- 2mm (US B/1) crochet hook.
- Approximately 20g (¾oz) of Scheepjes Catona, or similar 4-ply (fingering weight) yarn, in your chosen colour(s) for each pair
- Removable stitch markers or scrap yarn
- Hard cardboard or plastic for shoe inners (optional)

Instructions

Follow the instructions for Boots through to Round 5 of soles.

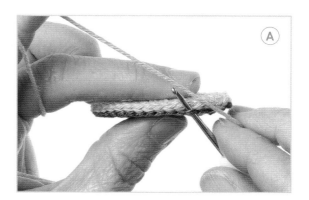

(A) Join yarn to the 5th front loop of under sole.

(B) **Round 1:** Ch 14, skip 29 sts, slst in next front loop of under sole, turn, dc 6 in next 6 front loops, ch 11, skip 16 sts, slst in next front loop, dc 6 in next 6 front loops, skip first st of ch, hdc 12 in ch, skip next st of ch and first dc, sc 4, skip next dc, hdc 10 in ch, skip next sts of ch and next dc, sc 4 in dc, skip last dc.

Fasten off and weave in ends (see General Techniques: Weaving in Ends).

Mary Janes

Materials

- 2mm (US B/1) crochet hook
- Approximately 10g (⅜oz) of Scheepjes Catona, or similar 4-ply (fingering weight) yarn, in your chosen colour(s) for each pair
- Removable stitch markers or scrap yarn
- Hard cardboard or plastic for shoe inners (optional)

Instructions

SOLES (MAKE 2)

You can make the bottom and top sole in two different colours to make your shoes look extra cool!

Using 2mm (US B/1) hook and chosen colour, ch 6.

Round 1 (RS): Sc 1 in second ch from hook, sc 3, sc 3 in next ch, sc 4 along opposite side of ch. (11 sts)

Place marker.

Round 2: Sc 3 in first st, sc 1, hdc 1, dc 1, dc 2 in next st, dc 3 in next st (this is the top st of your sole), dc 2 in next st, dc 1, hdc 1, sc 2. (17 sts)

Round 3: Sc 2 in next st, sc 3 in next st, sc 2 in next st, sc 4, [dc 2 in next st] 6 times, sc 4. (27 sts)

Round 4: Sc 2, sc 2 in next st, sc 3 in next st, sc 2 in next st, sc 8, [sc 2 in next st] 8 times, sc 7. (39 sts)

Round 5: Sc 5, slst in next st, stop the round here.

Fasten off and make another sole in the same way.

Crochet both soles together by holding them wrong sides together and slst through both soles (see General Techniques: Slip Stitch Seam).

> *You can insert a piece of cardboard or hard plastic between the two soles to make your shoe sturdier.*

Now connect your yarn to the back loop of first slst in the back of the soles to continue working on your shoe.

Place marker.

Round 1: Ch 1, sc 39.

Round 2: Hdc 12, [dc2tog] 8 times, hdc 11. (31 sts)

Round 3: Hdc 12, dc2tog, dc3tog, dc2tog, hdc 5, ch 8, skip 14 sts, slst into 15th st, sc 7 into ch, slst into ch, hdc 7.

Fasten off and weave in ends (see General Techniques: Weaving in Ends).

A doll can never have enough shoes!

LITTLE BOW (OPTIONAL)

Using 2mm (US B/1) hook and chosen colour, ch 3, dc 2 in first ch, ch 3, slst in first st of ch.

Repeat for the second half of bow.

Wrap the yarn around the middle of the bow a few times, fasten off and weave in ends (see General Techniques: Weaving in Ends).

Sew the bow onto the front of your shoe.

Essential aids

Sometimes our dolls need a little help too. In this chapter you'll find all the instructions you need to create those invaluable aids for your precious dolls.

AFOs (Ankle Foot Orthosis)

Materials

- 2mm (US B/1) crochet hook
- Approximately 5g (³⁄₁₆oz) of Scheepjes Catona, or similar 4-ply (fingering weight) yarn, in your chosen colour, plus oddments of a contrast colour for strap
- Removable stitch markers or scrap yarn

Instructions

SOLES

Using 2mm (US B/1) hook and chosen main colour, ch 6.

Round 1: Starting in second ch from hook, sc 4, sc 3 in next ch , sc 4 along opposite side of ch. (11 sts)

Place marker.

Round 2: Sc 3 in 1st st, sc 1, hdc 1, dc 1, dc 2 in next st, dc 3 in next st (the top st of your sole), dc 2 in next st, dc 1, hdc 1, sc 2. (17 sts)

Round 3: Sc 2 in next st, sc 3 in next st, sc 2 in next st, sc 4, [hdc 2 in next st] 6 times, sc 4. (27 sts)

Round 4: Sc 2, sc 2 in next st, sc 3 in next st, sc 2 in next st, sc 8, [sc 2 in next st] 8 times, sc 6. (39 sts)

Round 5: Sc 5, stop the round here.

Fasten off and weave in ends (see General Techniques: Weaving in Ends).

The sides of the AFOs are worked in rows, crocheting back and forth, **ch 1 (for sc) or ch 2 (for hdc) and turn** on each row.

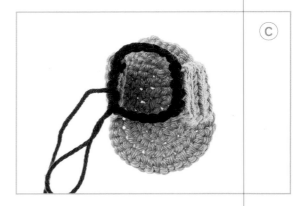

(A) **Row 1:** BLO: Join yarn to sixth st on the sole, ch 1 (does not count as st), sc 1 in same st as slst, sc 4, turn. (5 sts)

Rows 2 to 5: Ch 2 (does not count as st), hdc 5, turn.

Fasten off and weave in ends (see General Techniques: Weaving in Ends).

For the second side:

(B) **Row 1:** BLO: Join yarn to the 30th st of the sole, ch 1 (does not count as st), sc 1 in same st as slst, sc 4, turn. (5 sts)

Rows 2 to 5: Ch 2 (does not count as st), hdc 5, changing yarn colour on last yoh of last st of Row 5, turn.

Round 6: BLO: Sc 5, ch 7, sc 5 along the first side, ch 6, slst into first sc to close and **do not turn**. (10 sts and 13 ch)

Next round: Sc 5, hdc 7 along ch, sc 5, hdc 6 along ch. (23 sts)

(C) Fasten off and weave in end (see General Techniques: Weaving in Ends).

STRAP

Using 2mm (US B/1) hook and contrast colour, ch 27.

Row 1: Starting in third ch from hook, hdc 25. (25 sts)

Fasten off and leave a long tail for sewing.

FINISHING

Sew the strap closed with a few stitches to form a circle (see General Techniques: Sewing Joins) and sew around heel of AFO (on Round 2).

You can stretch the AFO a little bit to slide it over your doll's foot.

Leg prosthesis

Materials

- 2mm (US B/1) crochet hook
- Approximately 10g (⅜oz) of Scheepjes Catona, or similar 4-ply (fingering weight) yarn, in your chosen colour (you can use two different colours if desired)
- Removable stitch markers or scrap yarn
- 0.5mm (⅛₀in) wooden dowel
- Scrap of felt

Instructions

(A)— Choose if you want a right or left foot for your prosthesis and follow the basic instructions of that leg (see Basic Doll) through to Round 13. (16 sts)

Round 14: [Sc 2, invdec] 4 times. (12 sts)

Stuff leg.

Round 15: [Invdec] 6 times. (6 sts)

If desired, you can now switch to a contrast colour for the middle part of the leg.

Rounds 16 to 30: Sc 6.

> *You can adapt the height of the leg by adding or subtracting rounds.*

If desired, you can switch back to first colour for the top part of the leg.

Round 31: BLO: [Sc 2 in next st] 6 times. (12 sts)

Round 32: [Sc 1, sc 2 in next st] 6 times. (18 sts)

Round 33: [Sc 2, sc 2 in next st] 6 times. (24 sts)

Rounds 34 to 40: Sc 24.

Fasten off, close and weave in ends (see General Techniques: Weaving in Ends).

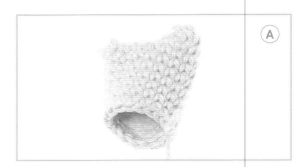

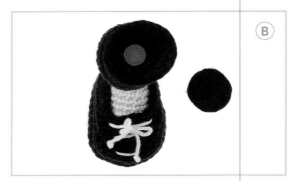

FINISHING

(B)—
(C)— Cut the dowel to size and insert into the leg. Place the magnet on top of the dowel, cut a small piece of felt and sew it on top of the magnet to keep it in place. Make sure the magnet is facing the right way!

Crutches

Materials

- 2mm (US B/1) crochet hook
- Approximately 10g (⅜oz) of Scheepjes Catona, or similar 4-ply (fingering weight) yarn, in your chosen colour (you can use two different colours if desired)
- 0.5mm (⅕₀in) wooden dowel

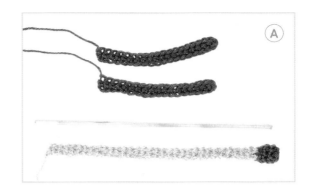

Instructions

Using 2mm (US B/1) hook and chosen colour, make a magic ring.

Round 1: Sc 8 into ring. (8 sts)

Round 2: BLO: Sc 8.

Round 3: Sc 8.

Change colour.

Rounds 4 to 35: Sc 8.

Next round: [Invdec, sc 2] twice. (6 sts)

Fasten off.

Cut dowel to size, insert into crutch, close and weave in ends (see General Techniques: Weaving in Ends).

STRAPS (MAKE 2)

Using 2mm (US B/1) hook and chosen colour, ch 19.

Round 1: Starting in second ch from hook, hdc 18. (18 sts)

Ⓐ — Fasten off, leave a long tail end.

Use tail end to sew ch into a circle (see General Techniques: Sewing Joins).

FINISHING

Sew one strap onto the top of the crutch between Rounds 33 and 34 and the other one between Rounds 28 and 29.

Wheelchair

Materials

- 2.25mm (US C/2) crochet hook
- Approximately 50g (1¾oz) of Scheepjes Catona, or similar 4-ply (fingering weight) yarn, in your chosen colours, plus oddments of silver, white and black for the wheels
- Hard cardboard or plastic
- 1.5mm (½₀in) wire
- Jewellery pliers
- 0.5mm (⅕₀in) wooden dowel
- Tapestry needle

Instructions

The wheelchair is made out of separate pieces that we will connect using slst or sc.

Each part is made up of two pieces that are crocheted together with a piece of cardboard or hard plastic in the middle to make the chair sturdier.

We will thread wires through the work to attach the wheels and make the handles for the wheelchair.

Seat

This part is worked in rows, crocheting back and forth, **ch 2 and turn** on each row.

Using 2.25mm (US C/2) hook, ch 24.

Row 1: Starting in third ch from hook, hdc 22, turn. (22 sts)

Rows 2 to 14: Ch 2 (does not count as st throughout), hdc 22, turn.

(A) Trace this piece onto cardboard or hard plastic and cut it out.

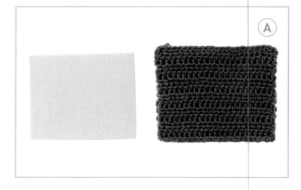

Row 15: BLO: Ch 2, hdc 22.

Rows 16 to 25: Ch 2, hdc 22, turn.

Fasten off.

Fold your work in half, the front loops of Row 15 will be in the centre on the outside of your work.

B — Join the yarn to one of the open sides but leave the first sts open (we will use this opening to insert a wire and dowel for the wheels later) and work an sc seam (see General Techniques: Single Crochet Seam) around the three open ends to close, sandwiching the piece of cardboard or plastic in between. Also leave the last sts open for the wire and dowel. Make sure you sc 2 sts in each corner.

BACK

This part is worked in rows, crocheting back and forth, **ch 2 and turn** on each row.

Using 2.25mm (US C/2) hook, ch 24.

Row 1: Starting in third ch from hook, hdc 22, turn. (22 sts)

Rows 2 to 17: Ch 2, hdc 22. turn.

C — Trace this piece onto cardboard or hard plastic and cut it.

Row 18: BLO: Ch 2, hdc 22, turn.

Rows 19 to 34: Ch 2, hdc 22, turn.

Close this piece the same way as the seat but don't leave any openings.

CONNECTING THE SEAT AND BACK

D —
E — Hold the back and seat together and join with slst (see General Techniques: Slip Stitch Seam) through the front loops (on Round 15 of seat and Round 18 of back) of both pieces.

Fasten off and weave in ends (see General Techniques: Weaving in Ends). You can use the ends to make a few extra sts where you connected both pieces.

Cut two 35cm (13¾in) pieces of 1.5mm (¹⁄₂₀in) wire and insert them into both sides of the chair, from the top of the back through to the bottom of the seat, leaving 7.5cm (3in) sticking out on the top and the rest on the bottom of the chair.

SIDES (MAKE 4)

This part is worked in rows, crocheting back and forth, **ch 2 and turn** on each row.

Using 2.25mm (US C/2) hook, ch 20.

Row 1: Starting in third ch from hook, hdc 18, turn. (18 sts)

Row 2: Ch 2 (does not count as st throughout), hdc 18, turn. (18 sts)

Row 3: Ch 2, hdc 16 , hdc invdec, turn. (17 sts)

Row 4: Ch 2, hdc2tog, hdc 15, turn. (16 sts)

Row 5: Ch 2, hdc 14, hdc2tog. (15 sts)

Fasten off and weave in ends (see General Techniques: Weaving in Ends).

(F)— Trace this piece onto cardboard or plastic and cut out.

(G)— Hold two pieces together and join the yarn. Work an sc seam around both pieces, sandwiching the cardboard or plastic in between, making sure to sc 2 in each corner.

Repeat for the second side piece.

CONNECTING THE SIDES TO THE CHAIR

(H)— Fold the chair at the connection row (you will be bending the wires as well). Place the (straight) corner of the side piece into the fold of the chair. Now join the yarn to the beginning of the side piece and the back of the chair and work a slst seam along that edge and the bottom edge (see General Techniques: Slip Stitch Seam) until you reach the end of the seat.

> *Make sure you don't close the small opening on the seat and slst only through the top layer of the seat on the joining stitches.*

Repeat this for the other side of the chair.

Footrest

TOP

This part is worked in rows, crocheting back and forth, **ch 2 and turn** on each row.

Using 2.25mm (US C/2) hook, ch 17.

Row 1: Starting in third ch from hook, hdc 15, turn.

Rows 2 to 4: Ch 2 (does not count as st throughout), hdc 15, turn. (15 sts)

Trace this piece onto cardboard or plastic and cut out.

Row 5: BLO: Ch 2, hdc 15, turn. (15 sts)

Rows 6 to 8: Ch 2, hdc 15, turn.

Fold your work in half, the front loops of Row 5 will be in the centre on the outside of your work.

Join the yarn and work an sc seam around the three open ends to close, sandwiching the piece of cardboard or plastic in between both sides. **Make sure you sc 2 sts in each corner.**

> *You can fold the footrest upwards to make a seat pillow for your wheelchair.*

BOTTOM

This part is worked in rows, crocheting back and forth, **ch 2 and turn** after each row.

Ch 17 with 2.25mm (US C/2) hook.

Row 1: Starting in third ch from hook, hdc 15, turn.

Rows 2 to 5: Ch 2 (does not count as st throughout), hdc 15, turn. (15 sts)

Trace this piece onto cardboard or plastic and cut out.

Row 6: BLO: Ch 2, hdc 15, turn. (15 sts)

Rows 7 to 10: Ch 2, hdc 15, turn. (15 sts)

Fold your work in half, the front loops of Row 6 will be in the centre on the outside of your work

Join the yarn and work an sc seam around the three open ends to close, sandwiching the piece of cardboard or plastic in between both sides. Make sure you sc 2 sts in each corner

(I) Now we will connect both parts of the footrest. Hold the front loops of Row 5 (of the top) and front loops of Row 6 (of the bottom part) together. Join the yarn and slst in both front loops to connect the parts,

(J) Place the finished footrest in the middle of the outer edge of the seat and sc 16 in the seat edge and the top of footrest to connect them.

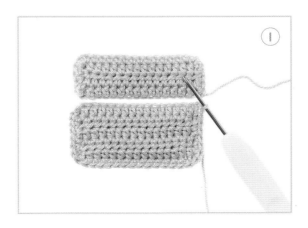

Big wheels (make 4)

Using 2mm (US B/1) hook and silver yarn, make a magic ring.

Round 1: Sc 8 into ring. (8 sts)

Change to white.

Round 2: [Sc 2 in next st] 8 times. (16 sts)

Round 3: [Sc 1, sc 2 in next st] 8 times. (24 sts)

Round 4: [Sc 2, sc 2 in next st] 8 times. (32 sts)

Round 5: [Sc 3, sc 2 in next st] 8 times. (40 sts)

Round 6: [Sc 4, sc 2 in next st] 8 times. (48 sts)

Round 7: [Sc 5, sc 2 in next st] 8 times. (56 sts)

Round 8: [Sc 6, sc 2 in next st] 8 times. (64 sts)

Round 9: [Sc 7, sc 2 in next st] 8 times. (72 sts)

Round 10: [Sc 8, sc 2 in next st] 8 times. (80 sts)

Switch to silver.

Round 11: BLO: [Sc 9, sc 2 in next st] 8 times. (88 sts)

Switch to black.

Round 12: BLO: Sc 88.

Fasten off and weave in ends (see General Techniques: Weaving in Ends).

1. Trace the wheel onto cardboard and mark the hole as well. Cut out two pieces and make the holes.

2. Hold the two crochet wheels with their wrong sides together sandwiching the two pieces of cardboard in between.

3. Connect black yarn around the back post of the first sts of the wheel that is facing you and hdc 1, then slst around the back post of the other wheel. Work your way around the wheels this way, alternating between hdc 1 around the back post of the front wheel and a slst around the back post of the back wheel.

4. Embroider the spikes onto the wheels with silver yarn (see General Techniques: Embroidery Stitches). Make eight spikes, going from the centre of the magic ring to the increase stitches of Round 10.

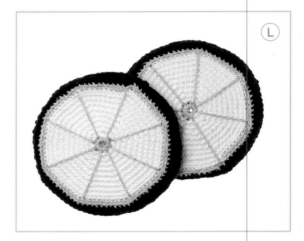

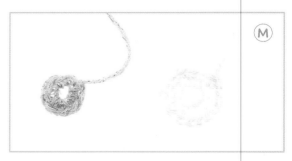

Small wheels (make 4)

Using 2mm (US B/1) hook and silver yarn, make a magic ring.

Round 1: Sc 8 into ring. (8 sts)

Change to white.

Round 2: [Sc 2 in next st] 8 times. (16 sts)

Round 3: [Sc 1, sc 2 in next st] 8 times. (24 sts)

Round 4: [Sc 2, sc 2 in next st] 8 times. (32 sts)

Switch to silver.

Round 5: BLO: [Sc 3, sc 2 in next st] 8 times. (40 sts)

Switch to black.

Round 6: BLO: Sc 40.

Fasten off and weave in ends (see General Techniques: Weaving in Ends).

1. Trace the wheel onto cardboard and mark the hole as well. Cut out two pieces and make the holes.

2. Hold the two crochet wheels with their wrong sides together sandwiching the two pieces of cardboard in between.

3. Connect black yarn around the back post of the first sts of the wheel that is facing you and hdc 1, now slst around the back post of the other wheel. Work your way around the wheels this way, alternating between hdc 1 around the back post of the front wheel and a slst around the back post of the back wheel.

4. Embroider the spikes onto the wheels with silver yarn. Make 8 spikes, going from the centre of the magic ring to the increase stitches of Round 4.

Wheel reinforcements

We'll crochet small circles to make the wheels sturdier.

OUTER REINFORCEMENT (MAKE 4)

Using 2mm (US B/1) hook and silver yarn, make a magic ring.

Round 1: Sc 8 into ring. (8 sts)

Fasten off and leave a long tail for sewing onto wheel.

INNER REINFORCEMENT (MAKE 4)

Using 2mm (US B/1) hook and white yarn, make a magic ring.

Round 1: Sc 8 into ring. (8 sts)

Round 2: [Sc 2 in next st] 8 times. (16 sts)

Fasten off and leave a long tail for sewing onto wheel.

MORE INNER REINFORCEMENT (MAKE 4)

Using 2mm (US B/1) hook and grey yarn, make a magic ring.

Round 1: Sc 8 into ring. (8 sts)

Fasten off and weave in ends (see General Techniques: Weaving in Ends).

FINISHING THE WHEELS

Sew the outer circles onto the exterior centre of all 4 wheels and the inner circles onto the inner centre of all 4 wheels.

O — **1.** Cut a 17cm (6¾in) piece of 1.5mm (½₀in) wire and a 12cm (4¾in) dowel or skewer and thread them through the back of the seat (where you left the openings before).

2. Thread two small grey reinforcement wheels on each side of the chair onto the dowel and wire.

P — **3.** Then thread the big wheels onto the dowel and wire, curl your wire in tightly making sure there're no sharp edges.

Finishing the small wheels and handles

We'll make the wheelchair handles and connect the small wheels to the wires that are sticking out on the bottom of the chair.

Q — Bend the top part of the wires that are sticking out of the back of the chair backwards at a straight angle and then bend about 2cm (¾in) of the edge double to form the handles.

HANDLES (MAKE 2)

Using 2mm (US B/1) hook, make a magic ring.

Round 1: Sc 6 into ring. (6 sts)

Round 2: [Sc 2, sc 2 in next st] twice. (8 sts)

Rounds 3 to 6: Sc 8. (8 sts)

Round 7: [Invdec, sc 2] twice. (6 sts)

R — Fasten off and leave a long tail for closing.

Pick up the front loops of your sts with a tapestry needle, slip the handles over the bended wire, pull your yarn to close the handles and sew the ends onto the back of the wheelchair very tightly (see General Techniques: Sewing Joins).

Weave in ends (see General Techniques: Weaving in Ends).

ATTACHING SMALL WHEELS

S — Bend the wires that are sticking out of the bottom of the seat down at a straight angle. Leave 4cm (1¾in) and bend the wire double for 0.5cm (¼in). Then bend it outwards at a straight angle.

Thread the wheels onto the wires and curl the ends of the wires in tightly, making sure there are no sharp edges sticking out.

WHEEL TOPPERS (MAKE 4)

Using 2mm (US B/1) hook and grey yarn, make a magic ring.

Round 1: Sc 6 into ring. (6 sts)

Round 2: BLO: Sc 6

Fasten off and leave a long tail.

T — Use your tapestry needle to pick up the front loops of all 6 st, slip onto the curled in wire ends and sew on tightly.

Heart decoration

Using 2mm (US B/1) hook, make a magic ring.

Round 1: Working into ring, (sc 1, hdc 3, dc 1, tr 1, dc 1, hdc 3, sc 1, slst back in magic ring)

Round 2: Sc 3 in first sc, sc 3 in next sc, sc 3, ch 2, slst back in first ch, sc 3, sc 3 in next 2 sts, slst in ring.

Round 3: Sc 10, ch 2 , slst back in first ch, sc 1 in same sts, sc 9, slst in beginning ring.

U — Fasten off and leave a long tail for sewing onto the back of the wheelchair.

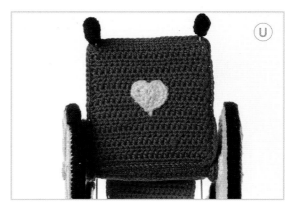

Glasses

Materials

- 1.2 mm (½₀in) wire
- Embroidery yarn
- Jewellery pliers
- A small round object of approximately 6cm (2½in) circumference to shape the glasses

Instructions

The glasses are not suitable for young children as they can pose a choking hazard and can easily bend and break.

Follow the steps below to make your glasses.

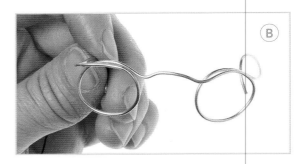

1. First cut a long piece of yarn, make a loop and thread it onto the wire. Pull the loop tight and turn in your wire, catching the thread into it so there won't be a sharp edge and your thread will be secured.

2. Shape the wire around your doll's right ear and measure the length until your doll's eye.

3. Using your jewellery pliers, bend your wire towards the doll's eyes.

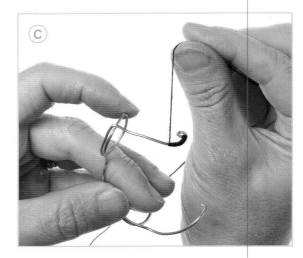

4. Now take a round object with a circumference of about 6cm (2½in) and shape the wire all around it for the first eye.

Make sure you bring the wire around the back of the glasses for both eyes!

5. Measure the distance until the second eye and twist the yarn around your round object again for the second eye.

6. Bend the wire towards and around the left ear.

7. Wrap your thread around the entire frame very, very tightly. You will need to thread your yarn onto a needle to be able to reach the whole frame.

8. Tie off the end and bend the wire around it to secure the yarn and round off your wire.

If you run out of yarn, just secure the end tightly and start a new piece of yarn.

You can change the shape of the glasses by bending your wire around different shaped objects like ovals.

Hearing aid

Materials

- 2mm (US B/1) crochet hook
- Scraps of Scheepjes Catona, or similar 4-ply (fingering weight) yarn, in your chosen colour

Instructions

(A)—Using 2mm (US B/1) hook and leaving a 10cm (4in) tail, make a magic ring. **Make the ring loose** (about 1 cm/⅜ in. across).

(B)—**Round 1:** Hdc 8 into ring.

(C)—Cut your yarn, place the hearing device over your doll's ear and pull the loop closed, Now you can sew it on tightly (see General Techniques: Sewing Joins).

Match the colour of the hearing aid to your doll's skin tone or make it stand out by using bright colours.

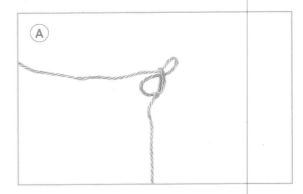

(A)

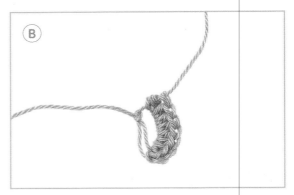

(B)

(C)

Cochlear implant

Materials

- 2mm (US B/1) crochet hook
- Scraps of Scheepjes Catona, or similar 4-ply (fingering weight) yarn, in your chosen colour (you can use two different colours if desired)

Instructions

SOUND PROCESSOR

Using 2mm (US B/1) hook and leaving a 10cm (4in) tail, make a magic ring. **Make the ring loose** (about 1 cm/⅜ in. across).

Round 1: Hdc 8 into ring, ch 15.

Fasten off and leave a long tail for sewing.

TRANSMITTER

Using 2mm (US B/1) hook, make a magic ring.

Round 1: Sc 6 into ring.

Fasten off and set aside, leaving a long tail for sewing onto the base of your transmitter.

Using 2mm (US B/1) hook, make a magic ring.

Round 1: Sc 6 into ring. (6 sts)

Round 2: [Sc 2 in next st] 6 times. (12 sts)

Round 3: [Sc 1, sc 2 in next st] 6 times. (18 sts)

(A) Fasten off and leave a long tail for sewing onto the doll's head.

FINISHING

(B) Sew the small circle of the transmitter onto the centre of the large circle. Then sew the chain of the sound processor onto the side of your transmitter.

(C) Now you can slip the sound processor over your doll's ear, pull the loop tight and sew the processor and transmitter onto your doll's head (see General Techniques: Sewing Joins).

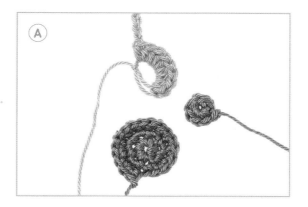

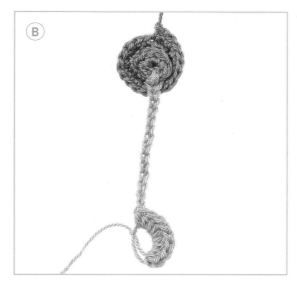

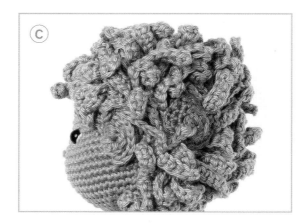

Feeding tubes & accessories

Materials

- 2mm (US B/1) crochet hook
- Approximately 5-10g (³⁄₁₆–³⁄₈oz) of Scheepjes Catona, or similar 4-ply (fingering weight) yarn, in your chosen colour (you can use two different colours for some pieces if desired)
- Removable stitch markers or scrap yarn
- Magnet(s)
- Scrap of felt

Instructions

If you would like to be able to remove and re-attach the feeding tube you can insert a little magnet into your doll's cheek/tummy before closing the head/body and sew the second magnet between the tube and the band aid/port.

Make sure you put the magnet in correctly and sew it in very tightly!

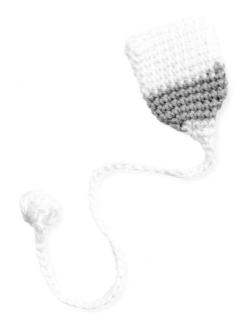

FEEDING BAG AND TUBE

Using 2mm (US B/1) hook and chosen colour, ch 10.

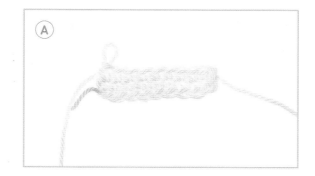

Round 1: Starting in second ch from hook, sc 8, sc 3 into next ch, sc 8 in opposite side of ch. (19 sts)

Place marker.

Round 2: Sc 2 in next st, sc 18. (20 sts)

Rounds 3 to 7: Sc 29.

Change colour (optional).

Rounds 8 to 10: Sc 20.

Round 11: Sc3tog, sc 7, sc3tog, sc 7. (16 sts)

Round 12: Sc3tog, sc 5, sc3tog, sc 5. (12 sts)

Change colour (optional).

Round 13: Sc3tog, sc 3, sc3tog, sc 3. (8 sts)

Round 14: Sc2tog, sc 1, sc3tog, sc 2. (5 sts)

Round 15: Invdec, sc 1, invdec. (3 sts)

Ch 45.

Fasten off and weave in ends (see General Techniques: Weaving in Ends).

BAND AID FOR NASAL FEEDING TUBE

Using 2mm (US B/1) hook and chosen colour, ch 3.

Round 1: Sc 1 in second ch from hook, sc 3 in next ch, sc 1 in opposite side of ch. (5 sts)

Round 2: Sc 3 in first st, sc 1, sc 3 in next st, stop the round here. (9 sts)

Fasten off and leave a long tail for sewing band aid onto ch.

FINISHING

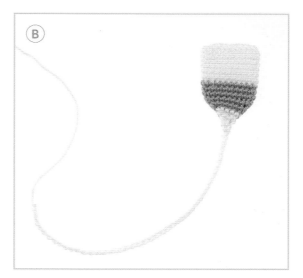

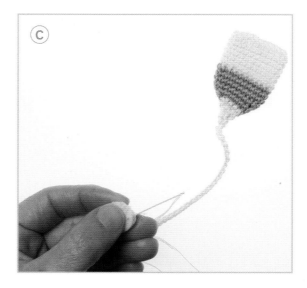

Sew the band aid onto the third st of the ch (see General Techniques: Sewing Joins). Cut a piece of felt the same size as the band aid and sew it onto the back of the band aid, placing the magnet between both layers (optional), or sew the band aid and tube onto your doll's cheek and nose.

PORT FOR ABDOMINAL FEEDING TUBE

Using 2mm (US B/1) hook and chosen colour, make a magic ring.

Round 1: Sc 5 into ring. (5 sts)

Round 2: BLO: Sc 5.

Round 3: BLO: Sc 2 in next st] 5 times. (10 sts)

Fasten off and weave in ends (see General Techniques: Weaving in Ends).

FINISHING

Pull the end of the ch from feeding bag through the hole of the port and sew on tightly. Cut a piece of felt the same size as your magnet and sew the port and felt together, sandwiching the magnet in the middle (optional). Or sew the port onto your doll's tummy where you want the feeding tube to be placed.

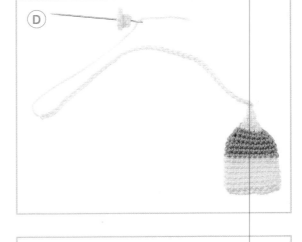

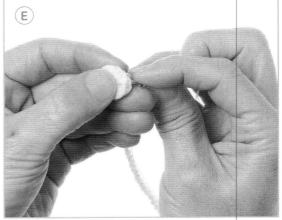

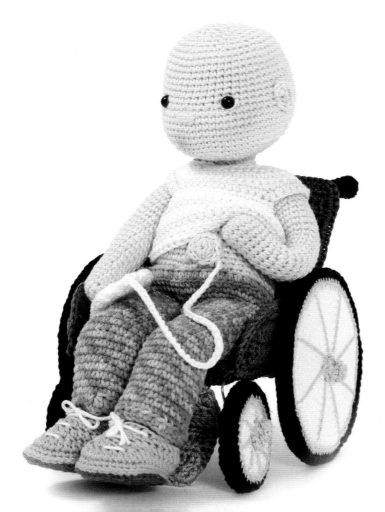

TRACHEOSTOMY TIE STRING FOR TRACHEA TUBE

Using 2mm (US B/1) hook and chosen colour, ch 13.

Round 1: Starting in second ch from hook, sc 12. (12 sts)

Fasten off and weave in ends (see General Techniques: Weaving in Ends).

FLANGE

Using 2mm (US B/1) hook and chosen colour, make a magic ring.

Round 1: Sc 6 into ring. (6 sts)

Round 2: BLO: Sc 6.

Round 3: BLO: [Sc 2 in next st] 6 times. (12 sts)

(F) Fasten off and leave a long tail for sewing onto tie string.

FINISHING

(G) Sew one side of the flange onto the tie string with a few visible straight stitches, place the string around the doll's neck and sew the other side of the flange onto the tie the same way.

You can make the tracheostomy removable by closing it in the back with a piece of yarn.

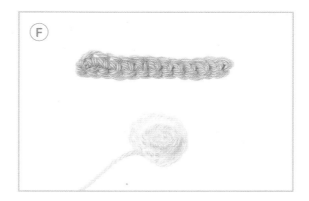

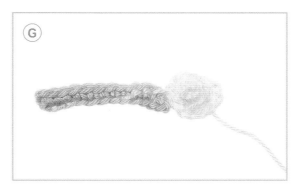

Assistance dog

Materials

- 2mm (US B/1) crochet hook
- Approximately 30g (1⅛oz) of Scheepjes Catona, or similar 4-ply (fingering weight) yarn, in your chosen colour (you can use two different colours if desired)
- Removable stitch markers or scrap yarn

> *If you would like your dog to be posable, insert a wire frame before you start stuffing. Make sure you turn in all the ends so there won't be any sharp edges.*

Instructions

You can make the tail and ears with fluffy yarn if you prefer.

HEAD

Using 2mm (US B/1) hook, make a magic ring.

Round 1: Sc 6 into ring. (6 sts)

Round 2: [Sc 2 in next st] 6 times. (12 sts)

Round 3: Sc 12.

Round 4: [Sc 3, sc 2 in next st] 3 times. (15 sts)

Rounds 5 to 6: Sc 15.

Round 7: [Sc 1, sc 2 in next st] twice, [sc 2 in next st] 7 times, [sc 1, sc 2 in next st] twice. (26 sts)

Round 8: Sc 4, [sc 2 in next st, sc 2] 6 times, sc 4. (32 sts)

Round 9: Sc 5, [sc 2 in next st, sc 3] 6 times, sc 3. (38 sts)

Rounds 10 to 15: Sc 38.

Place the safety eyes between Rounds 8 and 9 (see General Techniques: Attaching Toy Safety Eyes); there are 8 sts between the two eyes.

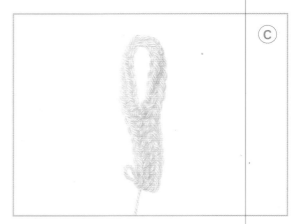

Round 14: [Sc 5, invdec] 5 times, sc 3. (33 sts)

Round 15: [Sc 4, invdec] 5 times, sc 3. (28 sts)

Round 16: [Sc 5, invdec] 4 times. (24 sts)

Round 17: [Sc 4, invdec] 4 times. (20 sts)

Stuff the head firmly and evenly.

Round 18: [Sc 3, invdec] 4 times. (16 sts)

Round 19: [Sc 2, invdec] 4 times. (12 sts)

Round 20: [Invdec] 6 times. (6 sts)

Ⓐ Fasten off, and weave in ends (see General Techniques: Finishing).

EARS (MAKE 2)

The ears are worked in rows, crocheting back and forth, **ch 1 and turn** on each row.

Using 2mm (US B/1) hook, make a magic ring.

Round 1: Sc 3 into ring. (3 sts)

Round 2: Sc 2 in first st, sc 1, sc 2 in last st. (5 sts)

Round 3: Sc 2 in first st, sc 3, sc 2 in last st. (7 sts)

Rounds 4 to 11: Sc 7.

Ⓑ Fasten off, leaving a long tail for sewing

Fold the top of the ears in half and sew onto the head on Round 13 (see General Techniques: Sewing Joins).

BODY

Using 2mm (US B/1) hook, ch 16.

Slst in first ch to form a circle, being careful not to twist your ch sts.

Ch 8.

You now have a loop with a chain attached to it. The loop is going to form the neck of your dog and the chain will become the back and body.

We are going to work around the loop and chain to form the body

Ⓒ **Round 1:** Sc 1 in second ch, sc 6, sc 16 around loop, sc 7 in opposite side of ch. (30 sts)

Place marker.

Round 2: [Sc 2 in next st, sc 2] 10 times. (40 sts)

Round 3: [Sc 3, sc 2 in next st] 10 times. (50 sts)

Round 4: [Sc 2 in next st, sc 2] 4 times, sc 29, [sc 2 in next st, sc 2] 3 times. (57 sts)

Ⓓ **Rounds 5 to 9:** Sc 57.

Move marker 2 sts forward and sc to marker.

Round 10: Sc 3, skip 10 sts, sc 7, skip 8 sts, sc 3, skip 8 sts, sc 7, skip 10 sts, sc 1. (21 sts)

Round 11: Sc 2, invdec, sc 5, invdec, sc 1, invdec, sc 5, invdec. (17 sts)

Round 12: Invdec, sc 6, invdec, sc 7. (15 sts)

Ⓔ Fasten off, leaving the gap open so you can stuff the legs later.

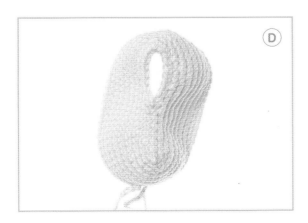

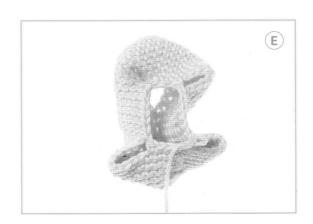

BACK LEGS

Round 1: Join yarn to the first st on the opening on one of the back legs and sc 10 around the opening, sc 3 in the gap. (13 sts)

Place marker.

Rounds 2 to 4: Sc 13.

Round 5: Sc 7, [invdec] 3 times. (10 sts)

Rounds 6 to 8: Sc 10.

Round 9: [Hdc 2 in next st, hdc 1] 5 times. (15 sts)

Round 10: [Sc 2 in next st, sc 2] 5 times. (20 sts)

Round 11: Sc 20.

Round 12: [Invdec] 10 times. (10 sts)

Round 13: [Invdec] 5 times. (5 sts)

Fasten off and weave in ends.

Repeat for the second back leg.

FRONT LEGS

Round 1: Join the yarn to the first st on the opening on one of the front legs and sc 8 around the opening, sc 2 in the gap. (10 sts)

Rounds 2 to 8: Sc 10.

Round 9: [Hdc 2 in next st, hdc 1] 5 times. (15 sts)

Round 10: [Sc 2 in next st, sc 2] 5 times. (20 sts)

Round 11: Sc 20.

Round 12: [Invdec] 10 times. (10 sts)

Round 13: [Invdec] 5 times. (5 sts)

Fasten off and weave in ends.

Repeat for the second front leg.

Stuff the bottom of the legs a tiny bit, then inset the wire frame (optional) and continue stuffing the legs and body very firmly.

Close the legs and weave in ends (see General Techniques: Weaving in Ends).

NECK

(J)— **Round 1:** Join the yarn to the first st in the neck opening, sc 16 around the neck, sc 1 in gap. (17 sts)

Fasten off, leaving a long tail to sew the head on.

Stuff the neck some more and sew the head on very tightly.

Close all gaps and weave in ends (see General Techniques: Weaving in Ends).

TAIL

(K)— Join the yarn to the first st of Round 2 of body, ch 12, slst in second ch from hook, sc 5, hdc 4, slst in last ch.

Fasten off and weave in ends (see General Techniques: Weaving in Ends).

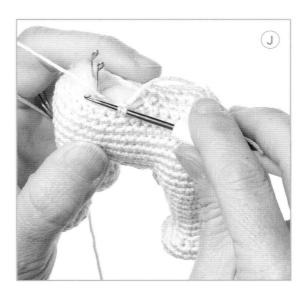

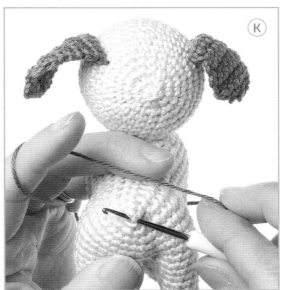

FINISHING

Embroider over the paws to create toes (see General Techniques: Embroidery Stitches).

(L)— Embroider a little triangle for the nose and two down slanting lines over the eyes for eyebrows.

VEST HARNESS

The vest is worked in rows, crocheting back and forth, **ch 1 and turn** on each row.

Using 2mm (US B/1) hook, ch 17.

Row 1: Sc 1 in second ch from hook, sc 5, dc 4, sc 6, turn. (16 sts)

Row 2: Ch 1, sc 6, hdc 4, sc 6, turn.

Row 3: Ch 1, sc 2 in first st, sc 14, sc 2 in last st, turn. (18 sts)

Row 4: Ch 1, sc 2 in first st, sc 16, sc 2 in last st, turn. (20 sts)

Row 5: Hdc 2 in first st, sc 18, hdc 2 in last st. (22 sts)

Switch colour (optional).

Starting on the right bottom corner of the vest, slst all around the edge. Don't cut the yarn, ch 16, sc 1 in the bottom left corner, then sc 16 back along the ch.

Fasten off.

Join the yarn to the right front corner, ch 17, sc 1 in left front corner, sc 17 back in ch.

Fasten off.

Place the vest on the dog's back.

Join the yarn to the second st between Rounds 3 and 4 of the vest, slst 7, ch 20, skip next 2 sts of vest, slst 8 in vest, ch 12, bring the ch around under the dog's belly, slst in first st between Rounds 3 and 4.

Fasten off and weave in all ends (see General Techniques: Weaving in Ends).

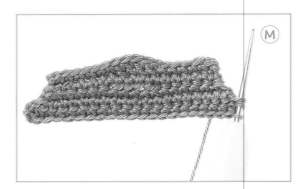

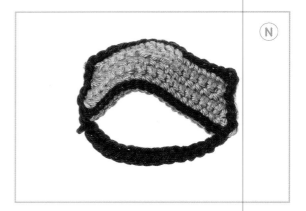

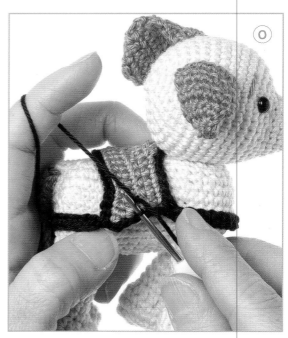

Bunny and teddy bear

Materials

- 2mm (US B/1) and 2.25 (US C/2) crochet hooks
- Approximately 20g (¾oz) of Scheepjes Catona, or similar 4-ply (fingering weight) yarn, in your chosen colours
- Removable stitch markers or scrap yarn
- Large cutlery fork

Instructions

FRONT PAWS (MAKE 2)

Using 2mm (US B/1) hook, make a magic ring.

Round 1: Sc 6 into ring. (6 sts)

Round 2: Sc 2 in next st, sc 5. (7 sts)

Rounds 3 to 5: Sc 7.

Round 6: Invdec, sc 5. (6 sts)

Ⓐ Fasten off and set aside. **Don't stuff!**

BACK PAWS AND BODY

Using 2mm (US B/1) hook, make a magic ring.

Round 1: Sc 7 into ring. (7 sts)

Round 2: Sc 7.

Round 3: [Sc 2, sc 2 in next st] twice, sc 1. (9 sts)

Round 4: Sc 9.

Slst in next st, fasten off and set aside.

Make second leg the same through to end of Round 4. (9 sts)

Now you'll connect both legs.

Ⓑ **Round 5:** Ch 2 and connect to first leg with sc 1 in first st, sc 8 around first leg, sc 2 along ch, sc 9 around second leg, sc 2 along opposite side of ch. (22 sts)

Place marker.

BODY AND HEAD

Round 1: Sc 6, [sc 2 in next st, sc 1] 5 times, sc 6. (27 sts)

Rounds 2 to 7: Sc 27.

Round 8: [Sc 3, invdec] 5 times, sc 2. (22 sts)

Round 9: [Sc 2, invdec] 5 times, sc 2. (17 sts)

Add some stuffing.

Round 10: [Invdec] 8 times, sc 1. (9 sts)

Round 11: [Sc 2 in next st] 9 times. (18 sts)

Round 12: [Sc 1, sc 2 in next st] 9 times. (27 sts)

Round 13: [Sc 2, sc 2 in next st] 9 times. (36 sts)

Rounds 14 to 20: Sc 36.

Round 21: [Sc 4, invdec] 6 times. (30 sts)

Round 22: [Sc 3, invdec] 6 times. (24 sts)

Add more stuffing.

Round 23: [Sc 2, invdec] 6 times. (18 sts)

Round 24: [Sc 1, invdec] 6 times. (12 sts)

Round 25: [Invdec] 6 times. (6 sts)

Ⓒ Fasten off, close all gaps and weave in ends (see General Techniques: Weaving in Ends).

BUNNY EARS (MAKE 2)

Using 2mm (US B/1) hook, make a magic ring.

Round 1: Sc 6 into ring. (6 sts)

Round 2: Sc 6.

Round 3: [Sc 2 in next st, sc 2] twice. (8 sts)

Round 4: [Sc 2 in next st, sc 3] twice. (10 sts)

Round 5: [Sc 2 in next st, sc 4] twice. (12 sts)

Rounds 6 to 14: Sc 12.

Round 15: [Invdec, sc 4] twice. (10 sts)

Round 16: [Invdec, sc 3] twice. (8 sts)

Round 17: Sc 8.

Fasten off, leaving a long tail for sewing onto the bunny's head.

TEDDY EARS (MAKE 2)

Using 2mm (US B/1) hook, ch 4.

Round 1: Sc 1 in 2nd ch from hook, sc 1, sc 3 in next ch, sc 2 in opposite side of ch. (7 sts)

Place marker.

Round 2: Sc 3 in first st, sc 2, sc 3 in next st, sc 3. (11 sts)

Round 3: Sc 1, sc 3 in next st, sc 5, sc 3 in next st, sc 3. (15 sts)

Round 4: Sc 15.

Fasten off, leaving a long tail for closing the bottom of the ear and sewing onto the teddy's head.

LITTLE BOW (OPTIONAL)

Using 2.25mm (US C/2) hook, ch 3, dc 2 in first ch, ch 3, slst in first st of ch.

Repeat for the second half of the bow.

Wrap the yarn around the middle of the bow a few times.

Fasten off and weave in ends (see General Techniques: Weaving in Ends).

FINISHING

Finish both bunny and bear as follows:

1. Sew the front paws on either side of the body on Round 23.

2. Pinch the ears closed and sew them on either side of the head on Round 21.

3. Embroider the eyes and little nose onto your bunny or teddy's face (see General Techniques: Embroidery Stitches).

4. Make a tiny little pompom for the bunny tail by winding yarn about 20 times around the tines of a fork. Cut a short length of yarn and thread through the middle gap below the wraps, take it right around the wraps and knot the ends very tightly. Remove from the fork, cut the wrap loops and fluff up the pompom. Sew it onto the back of the bunny.

5. You can sew on the little bow next to the ears or under the chin.

General techniques

Here you will find step-by-step instructions for the basic crochet stitches you will need. This section also includes the instructions for any special techniques mentioned in the patterns.

Crochet skills

Slip knot (or loop)

(A) Wrap your yarn around your crochet hook very loosely to form a loop. Pull the bottom yarn through the loop with your hook and pull closed. You have now created the first stitch of your new project.

Chain (ch)

(B) After creating a slip knot, wrap the yarn from back to front over your hook and draw through the loop, pull to close but not to tight. You have now created your first chain stitch. Make as many stitches as indicated in the pattern.

Slip stitch (slst)

(C) Insert your hook into the stitch as instructed on your work, wrap the yarn over your hook and pull through the stitch and the loop on your hook.

Magic ring

(D)
(E)
(F) This is the preferred method to start any crochet project. Start by forming a circle with your yarn, insert hook into circle, wrap your yarn over the hook and draw a loop through, but don't pull the circle tight. Now make a chain by wrapping your yarn over your hook and pulling it loosely through the loop on your hook. Next, make the required number of stitches into the beginning circle (as given in pattern). You can now pull the yarn tail to close the ring.

Single crochet (sc)

(G)
(H)
(I) This is the stitch we will use most in this book. Insert your hook into the next stitch (this may be a chain stitch or a stitch on a previous round), wrap your yarn over your hook and pull up a loop, there are two loops on your hook now. Wrap the yarn over your hook once more and pull it through both loops. This is one single crochet stitch. Insert your hook into the next stitch to continue.

Half double crochet (hdc)

(J) Wrap the yarn over your hook before inserting it into the next stitch. Wrap the yarn over your hook again and pull through the stitch, you now have 3 loops on your hook. Wrap the yarn over your hook and pull through all 3 loops.

Double crochet (dc)

(K)
(L)
(M) Wrap the yarn over your hook before inserting it into the next stitch. Wrap the yarn over your hook again and pull through the stitch, you now have 3 loops on your hook. Wrap the yarn over your hook and pull through 2 of the loops, you know have 2 loops on your hook. Wrap the yarn over your hook again and pull through both loops.

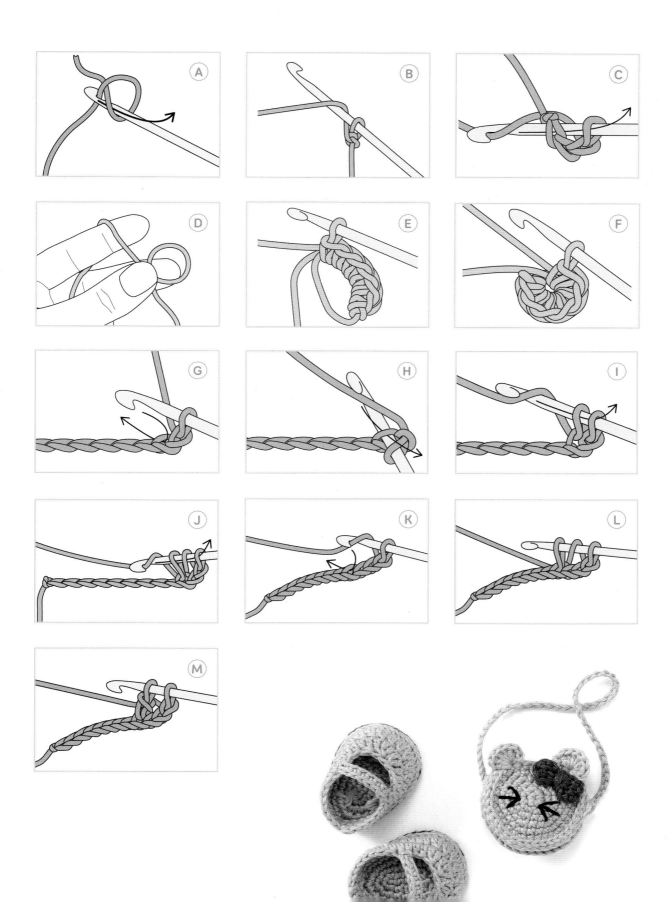

Treble (tr)

A — Wrap the yarn over your hook **twice** before
B — inserting it into the next stitch. Wrap the yarn
over your hook again and pull through the stitch,
you now have 4 loops on your hook. Wrap the
yarn over your hook and pull through 2 of the
loops, you know have 3 loops on your hook. Wrap
the yarn over your hook again and pull through 2
loops. Wrap the yarn over again and pull through
the 2 remaining loops.

Back loop only (BLO)

C — Insert your hook only into the **back** loop of the
next stitch.

Front loop only (FLO)

D — Insert your hook only into the **front** loop of the
next stitch.

Front post dc

E — Wrap the yarn over your hook. Instead of
F — inserting your hook into the loops of the next
stitch, insert your hook **around** the post right
under the loops, in the **front** of your work from
front to back to front, wrap the yarn over your
hook and pull up a loop. Now continue making
your dc as usual.

Back post dc

G — Wrap the yarn over your hook. Instead of
inserting your hook into the loops of the next
stitch, insert your hook **around** the post right
under the loops, in the **back** of your work from
back to front to back, wrap your yarn yarn over
your hook and pull up a loop. Now continue
making your dc as usual.

Reverse sc (crab stitch)

H — Insert your hook into the **previous** stitch on
I — your work from front to back and work a single
J — crochet as usual.

Invisible decrease with sc and hdc

K — This decreasing method is my preferred one,
L — it will give you an almost invisible, very neat
M — decrease: insert your hook into the **front loops** of
the next 2 stitches, wrap the yarn over your hook
and pull through both front loops, wrap the yarn
over your hook again and pull through both loops.

Do the same for hdc decrease, just wrap the
yarn over your hook before you insert it into the
2 front loops.

Increase 1

N — Sc/hdc/dc 2 stitches into the next stitch.

Decrease 1 (or sc2tog)

O — Insert your hook into the next stitch, yarn
over hook and pull up a loop, now insert
your hook into the next stitch, yarn over
hook and pull up another loop. You now
have 3 loops on your hook. Wrap the yarn
over your hook and pull through all 3 loops.

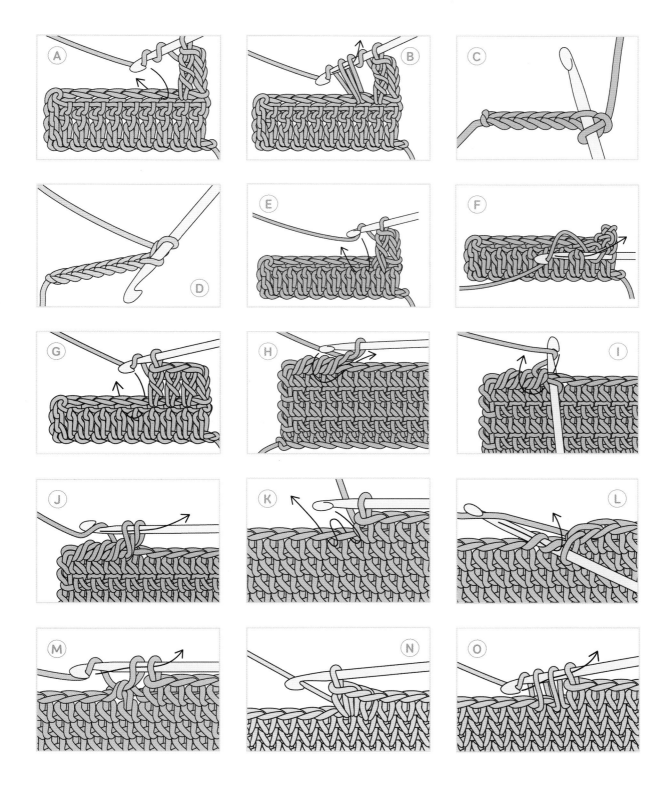

Assembly

Weaving in ends

(A) Thread the yarn onto your tapestry needle, pull the needle through 4-5 sts in one direction, rotate the needle and thread through 4-5 sts in opposite direction.

Slip stitch seam

(B)
(C) Insert your hook through both pieces of your work from front to back. Hold your yarn at the back of your work, yarn over and pull up a loop through both pieces and also through the loop that is on your hook.

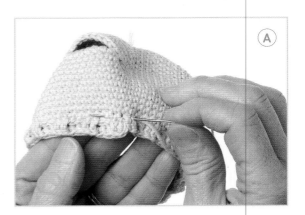

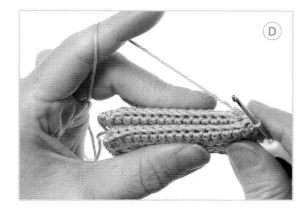

Single crochet seam

D
E Insert your hook through both pieces of your work from front to back. Hold your yarn at the back of your work, yarn over and pull up a loop through both pieces. There are now 2 loops on your hook. Yarn over and pull through both loops on your hook. Continue this way to close up the seam.

Sewing joins

F Thread a piece of yarn onto your tapestry needle (or use the yarn tail from your pieces) and use a whip stitch to close the gap or to securely attach your crochet pieces together.

Finishing

Attaching toy safety eyes

(A)
(B) Place the toy safety eye into the correct position and secure it by closing it with the flat side of the washer on the inside of your crochet piece. Make sure that you place the eyes correctly because once a washer is fixed in place it is impossible to remove.

Sewing on buttons

(C) Choose your buttons and thread the needle. Make a little knot at the bottom of the thread. Place the button in the correct place on your crochet work. Now thread the needle through the holes on your button a few times, then twist the yarn around the base of the button and tie off your yarn.

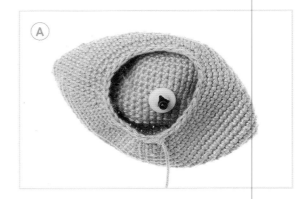

Embroidery stitches

STRAIGHT STITCH

(A) This is a basic sewing stitch that is created by passing the needle in and out of your work at a regular distance.

SATIN STITCH

(B) Satin stitch is used to cover a certain area in your crochet work (like noses and snouts). It is created by making a number of straight stitches very close together.

BACKSTITCH

(C) Pull up your thread through your work and go backwards for one stitch, then bring needle up, working forwards and in front of previous stitch. Repeat for as many stitches as needed.

BULLION STITCH

(D) Wrap the yarn around your needle a few times, insert your needle through your work from front to back, gently. This will create a small knot on the top of your work.

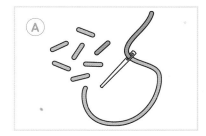

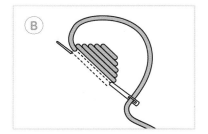

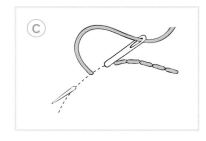

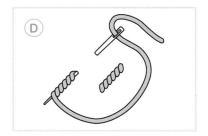

Adding those finishing touches will make your dolls look even more beautiful.

Templates

Each doll will need wire frames to support the body, leg(s), arm(s) and feet, as instructed within the pattern, along with a cardboard inner for shoe(s) to make them sturdy.

To help you with your frame making, I have provided a set of handy templates to help you shape your own pieces. These include the wire frame for legs and body, the wire frame for arms, and templates for feet and shoe sole. The templates are shown here at actual size, and printable versions can be downloaded from www.davidandcharles.com.

You can adapt your frames for limb loss by making the arms and legs to the specific length desired.

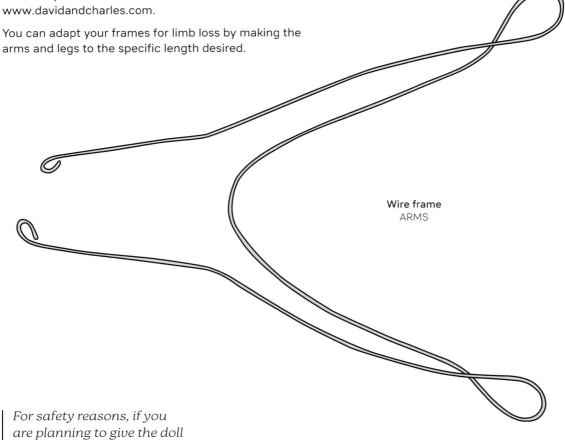

Wire frame
ARMS

For safety reasons, if you are planning to give the doll to a small child, you should not use wire frames.

*Make sure to curl in all
the ends of the wire so
there are no sharp edges.*

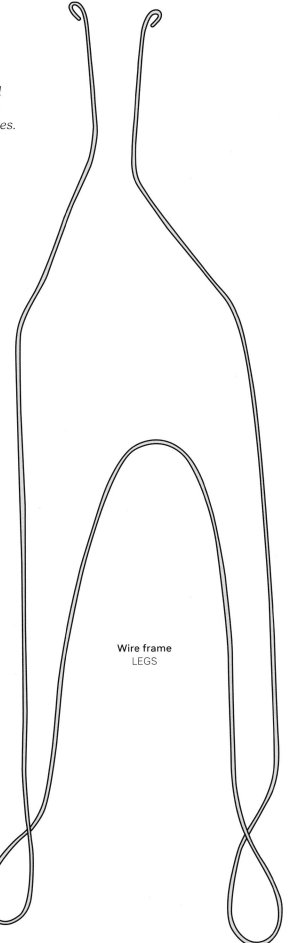

Wire frame
LEGS

Template
SHOE SOLES

About me

Hi, I'm Nathalie Amiel. My great aunt taught me how to knit and crochet when I was just a little girl and I started my online crochet and patterns shop when my sixth child was about one year old. I received a lot of requests to create dolls that were unique and different, from loving parents, grandparents and friends who couldn't find those special dolls anywhere else. Over the past seven years, I have made thousands of precious dolls; they have travelled around the world to reach their destinations and bring love and hugs to their new friends. When Sarah Callard reached out to me about writing a pattern book that would share my knowledge on how to create dolls that are different and special, I knew she had just made a huge difference in the world of doll-making. Now you too will be able to share your precious creations with your loved ones and believe me, there is no better feeling!

Suppliers

I used the following suppliers for the projects featured in this book:

Scheepjes (yarn): www.scheepjes.com

ChikaiMakers (safety eyes): www.etsy.com/uk/shop/ChikaiMakers

Marry You Store (crochet hooks): www.aliexpress.com/store/3220156

Amazon (craft magnets): www.amazon.com

Thanks

First I want to thank Sarah Callard, without whom this book would never have existed! I also want to thank the amazing people at David and Charles for having made this experience an absolute pleasure. Thank you, Jeni Chown, Lynne Rowe, Marie Clayton, Samantha Staddon, Anna Wade, Ali Stark, Prudence Rogers and Jason Jenkins.

I want to thank Ardon Bar-Hama, not only for setting me up with the most amazing mini studio where I can take the highest quality pictures only he knows how to create, but also for being there for me day and night, no matter where in the world, to help me out with technical emergencies.

A huge thank you goes to Scheepjes yarns! Thank you Sanne Smilda-Van Opstal and the whole team for supporting and believing in this project from the very first stitch until the very last one. Your yarns are simply a dream to work with and have made this project even more beautiful. Your kindness and generosity have moved me beyond words.

I want to thank all of you for your kind words of encouragement and support throughout the years, I feel truly blessed to be a part of this inspiring community.

A special thanks goes to my family; my parents and siblings, my son David – there are not enough words… without him none of this would ever have happened, my daughter Racheli, for always listening, and her husband Yagel, for bringing over my sweet one year old granddaughter who tested the dolls vigorously (I can assure you, readers, those dolls are sturdy!), my son Matania, for protecting me through thick and thin, my daughter Orya, for emergency testing my patterns, my daughter Aderet, for her unwavering support, and my daughter Avya, for playing with the dolls and helping me style them perfectly.

And last, my husband Didier, for helping me problem solve: technical difficulties with the computer, the workings of yarn wheelchairs, hooks, patterns, late night frustrations and tears, for never losing patience and for being so incredibly proud of me.

MAKING A DIFFERENCE

SINASRA is a non-profit voluntary organization where all funds are exclusively used to assist persons with albinism.

In Africa, living with albinism can be a death sentence. Adults, teenagers, but especially children and infants, can fall victim to brutal attacks and are at serious risk of contracting skin cancer. People with oculocutaneous albinism have little or no pigment in their hair, skin and eyes; thus they are visually impaired and very sensitive to the damaging effects of the sun.

SINASRA's primary concern is the survival of people with albinism, ensuring their livelihood and offering them a fair standard of living. The supply of protective clothing, sunscreen and dissemination of relevant information is aimed at preventing sun-related cancer, its complications and early death. I will donate money for every book I sell to **SINASRA**. By supporting **SINASRA** together, we will provide children who suffer from albinism with life saving skin tests, telescopic spectacles and dedicated care that enhances their possibility to live a safe and independent life.

www.sinasra.com

Photo credit: Patricia Willocq

Index

A DAVID AND CHARLES BOOK
© David and Charles, Ltd 2022

David and Charles is an imprint of David and Charles, Ltd
Suite A, Tourism House, Pynes Hill, Exeter, EX2 5WS

Text and Designs © Nathalie Amiel 2022
Layout and Photography © David and Charles, Ltd 2022 (except images on pages 124 and 125)

First published in the UK and USA in 2022

A catalogue record for this book is available from the British Library.

ISBN-13: 9781446309292 paperback
ISBN-13: 9781446381779 EPUB
ISBN-13: 9781446381762 PDF

This book has been printed on paper from approved suppliers and made from pulp from sustainable sources.

Printed in China through Asia Pacific Offset for:
David and Charles, Ltd
Suite A, Tourism House, Pynes Hill, Exeter, EX2 5WS

10 9 8 7 6 5 4 3

Publishing Director: Ame Verso
Senior Commissioning Editor: Sarah Callard
Managing Editor: Jeni Chown
Project Editors: Lynne Rowe and Marie Clayton
Head of Design: Anna Wade
Designer: Emma Teagle
Pre-press Designer: Ali Stark
Art Direction: Prudence Rogers
Photography: Jason Jenkins
Production Manager: Beverley Richardson

David and Charles publishes high-quality books on a wide range of subjects. For more information visit www.davidandcharles.com.

Share your makes with us on social media using #dandcbooks and follow us on Facebook and Instagram by searching for @dandcbooks.

Layout of the digital edition may vary depending on reader hardware and display settings.